CRIMINAL
CHILDREN

FAMILY HISTORY FROM PEN & SWORD

Tracing Secret Service Ancestors

Tracing Your Air Force Ancestors

Tracing Your Ancestors

Tracing Your Ancestors from 1066 to 1837

Tracing Your Ancestors Through
Death Records

Tracing Your Ancestors Through
Family Photographs

Tracing Your Ancestors Using the Census

Tracing Your Ancestors' Childhood

Tracing Your Ancestors' Parish Records

Tracing Your Aristocratic Ancestors

Tracing Your Army Ancestors – 2nd Edition

Tracing Your Birmingham Ancestors

Tracing Your Black Country Ancestors

Tracing Your British Indian Ancestors

Tracing Your Canal Ancestors

Tracing Your Channel Islands Ancestors

Tracing Your Coalmining Ancestors

Tracing Your Criminal Ancestors

Tracing Your East Anglian Ancestors

Tracing Your East End Ancestors

Tracing Your Edinburgh Ancestors

Tracing Your First World War Ancestors

Tracing Your Great War Ancestors:
The Gallipoli Campaign

Tracing Your Great War Ancestors: The Somme

Tracing Your Great War Ancestors: Ypres

Tracing Your Huguenot Ancestors

Tracing Your Jewish Ancestors

Tracing Your Labour Movement Ancestors

Tracing Your Lancashire Ancestors

Tracing Your Leeds Ancestors

Tracing Your Legal Ancestors

Tracing Your Liverpool Ancestors

Tracing Your London Ancestors

Tracing Your Medical Ancestors

Tracing Your Merchant Navy Ancestors

Tracing Your Naval Ancestors

Tracing Your Northern Ancestors

Tracing Your Pauper Ancestors

Tracing Your Police Ancestors

Tracing Your Prisoner of War Ancestors:
The First World War

Tracing Your Railway Ancestors

Tracing Your Royal Marine Ancestors

Tracing Your Rural Ancestors

Tracing Your Scottish Ancestors

Tracing Your Second World War Ancestors

Tracing Your Servant Ancestors

Tracing Your Service Women Ancestors

Tracing Your Shipbuilding Ancestors

Tracing Your Tank Ancestors

Tracing Your Textile Ancestors

Tracing Your Trade and Craftsmen Ancestors

Tracing Your Welsh Ancestors

Tracing Your West Country Ancestors

Tracing Your Yorkshire Ancestors

CRIMINAL CHILDREN

*Researching Juvenile Offenders
1820–1920*

Emma Watkins and Barry Godfrey

Pen & Sword
FAMILY HISTORY

AN IMPRINT OF PEN & SWORD BOOKS LTD
YORKSHIRE – PHILADELPHIA

First published in Great Britain in 2018 by
PEN & SWORD FAMILY HISTORY
An imprint of Pen & Sword Books Ltd
Yorkshire – Philadelphia

Copyright © Emma Watkins and Barry Godfrey, 2018

ISBN 978-1-52673-808-0

Typeset by Concept, Huddersfield, West Yorkshire.
Printed and bound in England by CPI Group (UK) Ltd, Croydon, CR0 4YY.

Pen & Sword Books Ltd incorporates the imprints of Aviation, Atlas, Family
History, Fiction, Maritime, Military, Discovery, Politics, History, Archaeology,
Select, Wharncliffe Local History, Wharncliffe True Crime, Military Classics,
Wharncliffe Transport, Leo Cooper, The Praetorian Press, Remember When,
White Owl, Seaforth Publishing and Frontline Publishing.

For a complete list of Pen & Sword titles please contact
PEN & SWORD BOOKS LTD
47 Church Street, Barnsley, South Yorkshire, S70 2AS, England
E-mail: enquiries@pen-and-sword.co.uk
Website: www.pen-and-sword.co.uk
or
PEN & SWORD BOOKS
1950 Lawrence Rd, Havertown, PA 19083, USA
E-mail: uspen-and-sword@casematepublishers.com
Website: www.penandswordbooks.com

CONTENTS

CHAPTER ONE

INTRODUCTION

This book explores how 'offending' children were dealt with from the early nineteenth century to the early twentieth century. Over this 100-year period, ideas about how children *should* behave, and how they should be corrected when they misbehaved, changed dramatically. Indeed, it was the period in which 'juvenile delinquency' is said to have been 'invented', when the problems of youth crime and youth gangs developed, and society began to ask, for the first time, how do we stop criminal children from developing into criminal adults? There were various experiments in reformation, ranging from transporting child convicts to Australia, to the creation of separate juvenile prisons, and the establishment of reform schools. But did any of these things actually work? This book reveals the lives of some of the thousands of children who were transported, imprisoned or kept in reformatory or industrial schools for years, to see how their lives turned out in reality.

In October 1872 the *Morpeth Herald* reported that two boys had been apprehended for housebreaking. At Newcastle Crown Court Richard Clement Fisher and Henry Leonard Stephenson were charged with housebreaking and theft. Henry, whose picture appears on the cover of this book, was a 12-year-old dark-haired boy with hazel-coloured eyes. In the dock he pulled himself up to his full height of 4 foot 5 inches to hear the defence and prosecution speeches. During the previous six weeks, several unoccupied houses in the area had been broken into and their contents ransacked. Detective Anderson stated in his evidence that he had spied the two prisoners acting suspiciously and he marched them to their parents' houses. Turning out the boys' pockets revealed a bunch of keys. One opened a small wooden box which contained some money and jewellery that had been stolen from the houses. In front of his grandmother, who was his guardian, and the detective, Henry admitted that he and his mate were responsible for the break-ins.

In court, Richard Fisher's parents said that all the stolen property had been restored and that Richard would be sent away to serve in the Navy. The parents asked for a merciful consideration of the case. They claimed that the boys had really broken into these houses, not so much for the purpose of stealing the property, as from an idea that they were doing heroic and manly acts, having perhaps been reading the wrong sort of books. Witnesses were called, who gave the boys good characters, and it was stated that Henry Stephenson would be sent to India if he was released from the court. The prosecutors stated that they did not wish to continue the case, but it was out of their hands as by then the court had completely taken charge of the proceedings. Richard Fisher was sentenced to four months' imprisonment with hard labour, and Henry Stephenson to two months' imprisonment. The court was probably convinced the boys would leave the country, and that is why the Judge did not send them to a reformatory where they would have stayed for a number of years.

The courts had many options when it came to sentencing children in this period. Many of the boys and girls mentioned in this book would have been confined to reformatories or industrial schools in order to give them a measure of punishment but also to train them in employment skills (and sometimes just to take them away from abusive or neglectful home lives); others were simply imprisoned, fined, or put on probation. A generation earlier, and the boys could have been sent to a foreign country for their punishment. We will examine the lives of children who were transported to Australia as convicts (a system which lasted from 1788 to 1868), and those who suffered other punishments. We will also explain how we know so much about the young people in this book, and how contemporary sources can be used to reconstruct the lives of boys and girls who got into trouble with the courts in the Victorian and Edwardian periods.

But what happened to Henry? Piecing together information from Victorian newspapers, genealogical data and speculation on various websites, we know that Henry's grandfather was a chemist who had been Superintendent of Factories for the East India Company in Bihar. His grandmother was a doctor's daughter. Henry's father, Henry Layton Stephenson, was a railway worker who had remarried after his wife (Henry's mother) died when Henry was just 3 years old. When he remarried, he left Henry behind with his first wife's parents when he emigrated to New Zealand in 1874. After serving his sentence, and after his grandmother's death, Henry also emigrated to Ashburton in New Zealand to join his father and his step-sisters in 1878. The whole family prospered in New Zealand. Henry's father rose to a high position at work and in the Freemasons, and Henry himself never committed another crime. His spell in prison seems to have been a salutary experience.

The concept of 'juvenile delinquency' was already established by the time Henry was convicted, and Chapter Two reveals the birth of this concept. It describes the origins of 'youth crime' in the early nineteenth century, and how children, particularly working-class children, were caught up in police campaigns against public disorder. As the century progressed, fears of juvenile gangs caught the public imagination, and the lives of real and imagined gang members were splashed over the pages of the newspapers. Press attention did not subside in the twentieth century, however, and this chapter discusses how moral panics have coloured our views about youth crime for decades.

Following conviction in the courts came punishment. Chapter Three describes the various types of punishment that were imposed on child offenders, from transportation to the Australian colonies and imprisonment, to care and control regimes in reformatories and industrial schools. We end the chapter with a look at the borstal system created in 1902 to deal with the worst of the young offenders.

The following chapter, Chapter Four, is critical. It explains how we can find out more about the lives of young offenders from contemporary archival and digital records, how that data can be put together to make sense of a young person's troubled life, and what ethical considerations should be kept in mind when we research the lives of young people in the nineteenth and early twentieth centuries.

Having discussed how we can use historical documents to reconstruct lives, we then look at a selection of children's lives in Chapter Five. We examine their lives before they were caught up in the criminal justice system, their experiences under punishment, and how their lives unfolded after they were released. Whilst some 'offending' children went on to lead very normal and routine lives, others had dramatic and troubled histories, which are sad, fascinating and also illuminating.

The Conclusion which rounds off the book is followed by a selection of further reading for those who want to learn more about the history of young people, youth crime and the punishment of child offenders in the nineteenth and twentieth centuries.

CHAPTER TWO

THE CONCEPT OF 'JUVENILE DELINQUENCY'

Today the peak age of offending is 18, the same as it was for men in the eighteenth century. For women, it is much lower today (15) than it was in the eighteenth and nineteenth centuries. Most offenders today fall into the category known by the criminal justice system as 'youth offending', where anyone under the age of 18 is dealt with in a juvenile court and anyone under 21 serves a custodial sentence in a young offenders' institution rather than in an adult prison. However, despite the fact that most offenders tend to concentrate their offending in their late teens, society, politicians and the media all seem to spend a disproportionate amount of time focusing on young offenders between the ages of 10 (the age of criminal responsibility) and 16. Teenage offenders have long captured the public imagination. Indeed, we don't have to look very hard to find reports of unruly, rude and criminal children in the Victorian newspapers. This report was printed in *Lloyd's Illustrated Newspaper* on 13 April 1851:

'A Juvenile Highway Robber' – an impudent Jack Shepherd [Jack was a notorious burglar who escaped from prison on two occasions] belonging to a desperate gang of juvenile thieves infesting the borough ... was charged with knocking down a lad and stealing sixpence and a basket in the public highway. A witness saw the 12-year-old perpetrator snatch the basket, knock the victim to the ground, give him a good kicking, and run away, and went to fetch a constable. The police officer from M Division in Southwark 'having knowledge of the prisoner, found him in "Thieves Kitchen", in the Mint, where the gang of thieves to which the prisoner belonged, frequented'.

Newspaper reports did not only bring us news about notorious habitual offenders. The *Sunday Times* on 12 October 1856 reported:

John Clark, a smart-looking lad, 16 years of age, was charged with stealing some beef. When he was apprehended by the butcher, the prisoner said 'Let me go, I won't do it again', but he was handed over to a police constable. The defendant refused to say where he was living so that his friends did not discover his plight. He appeared to be living rough, getting money where he could. The magistrate asked him what he had intended to do with the beef. 'Why, eat it, to be sure.' He was sentenced to four months' imprisonment in Wandsworth House of Correction. 'The prisoner was then led away by the gaoler, laughing'.

There were so many reports of teenage thieves such as those above that readers of newspapers in the nineteenth and early twentieth centuries could be forgiven for thinking that committing theft and violence was a natural life-stage for working-class children. How and why did it become a common expectation that a considerable number of children would naturally resist authority, cause mischief and break the law? It wasn't always that way.

The Legal Definition of Childhood

Legal doctrine in the eighteenth century determined that children aged 6 and younger were not capable of doing anything truly evil and could not, therefore, be held responsible for their actions in court (legally this was called *doli incapacitas*). Above the age of 7, children were granted the same status as adults: they could drink alcohol, gamble and be employed, and were therefore subject to the same level of legal responsibility as adults. However, this shifted over time. It was still the case that children aged under 7 could not be prosecuted, but in the nineteenth century children aged between 7 and 14 could be prosecuted only if the prosecutor could convince the judge and jury that the child in the dock knew they were committing a crime (*doli capax*) rather than just being 'naughty'. This still meant that young children could end up in prison, or could be transported to the American or Australian colonies (as happened to William Gadsby, Letitia Padwick and Ellen Miles, see Chapter Five), or, in some cases, could be sent to the gallows for execution. We will explore the punishments meted out to children later (see Chapter Three), but how did society come to think that young children deserved to be prosecuted and punished?

Good and Bad Children

Following the end of the Napoleonic Wars in 1815, respectable society became concerned about large numbers of decommissioned soldiers who were now unemployed and roaming around the country. Young men, physically tough and well-used to violence, were 'tramping' through towns and cities looking for work. They also fought with each other and with locals, got drunk, stole or damaged property, and slept out in the open. They were not popular. At about the same time as people were generally uneasy about lawlessness, 'The Committee for Investigating the Causes of the Alarming Increase of Juvenile Delinquency in the Metropolis' produced its report (in 1816).

It was one of the first times that the phrase 'juvenile delinquency' was used. The report found that:

> Juvenile Delinquency existed in the metropolis to a very alarming extent; that a system was in action, by which these unfortunate Lads were organised into gangs; that they regularly conspired together in public houses, where they planned their enterprises, and afterwards divided the produce of their plunder.

This sounded more like muscular young ex-soldiers than anything else, so how did the term 'juvenile delinquent' come to be applied to kids hanging round on street corners? The first clue is in the word 'delinquency'. From which ideal were these children delinquent, what were they not able to live up to?

Although children were treated as 'small' or 'young' adults in the eighteenth century, nineteenth-century society was beginning to consider a more refined concept of childhood. From the 1820s and 1830s onwards, children were increasingly removed from the workplace (especially by the Factory Acts which took young children out of the unhealthy and dangerous textile mills). They were increasingly required to undergo some form of elementary education, and were becoming the focus of commercial activity by the 1820s and 1830s. Shops sold toys, and children's books were published in increasing numbers. These books romanticised the idea of childhood. For example, Charles Kingsley's *The Water Babies* was published in 1863 and Lewis Carroll's *Alice's Adventures in Wonderland* two years later. When *Peter Pan*, the story of the boy who never grew up, was written by J.M. Barrie in 1902, it became a firm favourite with children and adults alike. All of these books helped to celebrate the idea of childhood (of a particular type). They were aimed at and made for children who deserved them: that is to say, they were meant for good, dutiful, polite and 'sweet' children. They were not meant for children whose parents could not afford to buy books or toys (which was the majority of working-class parents).

Children who could not live up to the 'ideal' concept of childhood were perceived to be delinquent, troublesome, rude and, in some cases, criminal. As Chapter Three explains, the Victorians put a great deal of effort into sorting out which children could be rehabilitated and which could not. Although children were thought to be more malleable and reformable than adults, there were still some children (boys usually) who were thought to be incapable of reform, as

The painting 'Bubbles' by John Everett Millais (1886) was subsequently used as an advert for Pears soap in the 1890s. (*Wikimedia Commons*)

Chapter Three shows. And after 1837, society could begin to visualise these 'criminal' children thanks to the most famous author in the world at that time.

Charles Dickens, who himself was sympathetic to the plight of poor and working-class children, was nevertheless central to the creation of the concept of delinquency. *Oliver Twist,* published in 1837, featured a gang of young thieves controlled by their puppet-master Fagin. Their juvenile leader was the Artful Dodger, described here:

> He was a snub-nosed, flat-browed, common-faced boy ... as dirty a juvenile as one would wish to see; but he had about him

The Artful Dodger. (*Wikimedia Commons*)

all the airs and manners of a man. He was short for his age: with rather bow-legs, and little, sharp, ugly eyes ... He wore a man's coat, which reached nearly to his heels. He had turned the cuffs back, half-way up his arm, to get his hands out of the sleeves: apparently with the ultimate view of thrusting them into the pockets of his corduroy trousers; for there he kept them. He was, altogether, as roystering and swaggering a young gentleman as ever stood four feet six.

The Artful Dodger shared many characteristics with poor children, especially those who were orphans, had been deserted by their parents, or were just generally neglected. Street children grew up quickly, so not only had the 'airs and manners of a man' but also had to fend for themselves. In an age without help from the State (other

David Lloyd, arrested for larceny in 1902.
(*Tyne and Wear Archives,* *DX1388-1-9*)

than the looming menace of the workhouse), children stole food and clothes in order to survive, and lived rough or in cheap lodging houses (which were full of sexual danger, dirt and disease).

Dickens' novel was supposed to act as a warning to society: this is what could happen if disadvantaged children are not looked after. However, the Victorian readership mainly saw *Oliver Twist* as a warning against rapacious, thieving, dreadful, but very street-smart, children. By the 1850s the newspapers were also full of stories of rampaging children, and society would worry about delinquent young people for at least the next 150 years. But all of this was not caused just by worries about demobbed young soldiers and the words of Charles Dickens. Other factors were also evident in the early to mid-nineteenth century. They all stoked the fire.

The Youth 'Crisis' of the Early to Mid-Nineteenth Century

During the nineteenth century Britain underwent a transformation. The industrial revolution created towns, and towns became cities teeming with thousands of incomers and new settlers. It was estimated that a thousand people a week flooded into London looking for jobs created by the new industrial economy. People who had grown up in villages, with friends and family nearby, were now surrounded by strangers and unfamiliar faces and places. The old order seemed to be crumbling. There was a concern that people were no longer going to church and that young people no longer knew the stories in the Bible. The noted social investigator and journalist Henry Mayhew commented that some children did not know the name of their Saviour, Jesus Christ. Religious and evangelical societies were formed to combat the lack of 'moral fibre' in the young, and the subject was debated vigorously in the newspapers and in Parliament. Fears remained, however, that children were not learning good manners, nor receiving a Christian education, nor adopting any of the normal rules of behaviour that society required.

Industrialisation was also blamed for the lack of available moral teachers – starting a long debate on working mothers which continues to this day. The fact that women were able to (and for the majority of families needed to) work in the new mills and factories meant that they were absent from the family home, and also (as we will see later in the chapter) very visible in society. 'Factory women

15

make bad mothers' was the predominant message in many articles and newspaper reports. Henry Mayhew, ever ready to comment on society's perceived problems, stated: 'Parental instruction; the comforts of a home, however humble ... the influence of a proper example; the power of education; the effect of useful amusement; are all denied to them.' It is true that the removal of children from the workplace, and the lack of a daily school regime until later in the century, meant that children were more free to roam. Children with parents who were struggling to hold down jobs, or who were absent from the family home, were especially free to wander. And that made them vulnerable to arrest.

Destitute or neglected children roaming the streets without any parental care or control were in danger of breaking new laws that had been brought in to keep public order in the growing towns and cities. The Vagrancy Act of 1824, for example, was brought in to control the demobbed soldiers, but caught up in its net destitute and disorderly children. The Malicious Trespass Act of 1829 empowered magistrates to deal with damage or trespass on private and public property – just the sort of thing that children were likely to do, particularly when 'scrumping' for apples (picking fruit from a farmer's trees, or from a landed estate's gardens) or picking up bits of coal from the slag heaps (a valuable source of 'free' heating). The Vagrancy and Malicious Trespass legislation may not have been specifically aimed at controlling children, but it did result in large numbers of children ending up in trouble for comparatively minor crimes.

With delinquent children regarded as visible signs of 'trouble', the new police forces introduced from 1835 were keen to sweep them off the streets and into the courts. Not only was it a way of proving how effective they were at controlling crime, it also seemed to make the police more popular with the general population. Since they were paid for by taxation, and mainly arrested the working classes, police officers were not always popular figures on the local streets, but every class of person seemed happy to see the local 'Bobby' marching off the local young troublemakers.

At the same time as policing was being reorganised, so was the court system. The 1847 Juvenile Offenders Act allowed victims of crime to prosecute children aged under 14 in the cheap local magistrates' courts, rather than in the expensive quarter sessions courts (most victims had to pay to bring a defendant to court in those days). The 1855 Criminal Justice Act then moved all theft of property valued at five shillings or less (the sort of thefts committed by juveniles) to the minor courts too. These changes to the way in which young people and minor offending were dealt with by the courts resulted in a huge rise in the numbers of juveniles being prosecuted. As would be expected, most people assumed this was due to more children committing more crimes, rather than being the result of new legislation, or the introduction of easier, cheaper and quicker ways of dealing with delinquent youths. For this reason, many researchers now talk about the 'invention' of juvenile delinquency in the early to mid-nineteenth century, rather than a real rise in juvenile offending.

The 'Invention' or the 'Discovery' of Juvenile Delinquency?

So, was juvenile delinquency simply a myth? The eminent criminologists Sir Leon Radzinowicz and Roger Hood thought so. They remarked that the 'concept of the juvenile offender, with all that implies for penal policy, is a Victorian creation'. Normal youthful activities were made criminal in this period, and therefore a whole raft of young people were labelled and treated as criminals. There was no sudden rise in criminal behaviour by the young – it was simply the result of the criminalisation of traditional youthful activities.

This conclusion may be a bit too simplistic. Whether or not it was because of new legislation and court procedures, a lot of juveniles were prosecuted in this period. Annual criminal statistics were published from 1857, and they showed an increase in crime in general, and by youths in particular. Evidence from the newspapers suggests that there was a real rise in juvenile offending. London seemed plagued by juvenile pickpockets.

Just as Dickens had done in the 1830s, one social investigator, Henry Mayhew, described a 15-year-old pickpocket for his readers in the mid-nineteenth century:

> ragged, dirty, and very thin overcoat under which was another thin coat, so arranged that what appeared rents – and indeed were rents [tears in the fabric] were slits through which the hand readily reached the pockets of the inner garment, and could there deposit any booty.

Target areas for pickpockets were theatres, fairs, marketplaces, shopping areas and crowded public streets. Silk handkerchiefs, pocket-

17

watches and purses were all high-value small objects that could be quickly spirited away by a skilful pair of juvenile hands. They were also easily sold on, and returned a good profit for proficient pick-pockets like 17-year-old Samuel Galling. In 1811 he was part of a threesome who relieved Mr Stafford Cooper of his silk handkerchief in a sophisticated operation. At the Old Bailey, the victim said that he:

> felt my pocket move, I put my hand to my pocket, and missed my handkerchief, the prisoner passed me, I suspected he took my handkerchief, I stepped on very quick, touched the prisoner on the shoulder, and said, 'you have got my handkerchief in your hand'; he said 'no it is not your handkerchief,' I said it was, I put my hand upon it, he said some other person gave it him ... there were three or four people buzzing about him ... two or three young men kept buzzing about, we put him in an Hackney coach, he begged that I would not appear against him. He said he was a very good young man, and it was his first offence.

Samuel put up a spirited defence, stating in his testimony:

> In the afternoon of that day, I had been to see a relation, in my way home I met an old school-fellow whom I had not seen some years, and on our coming up Catherine Street in the Strand, my school-fellow put a handkerchief in my hand, and before I had time to ask him the reason of so extraordinary a circumstance, the prosecutor came up and asked me for the handkerchief, upon which I was alarmed, and had no doubt he had stolen it from the prosecutor; upon the prosecutor's attempting to take me, I ran away; I do solemnly declare my running away was not from a consciousness of guilt, but for my unfortunately happening to be with one who had so departed from moral honesty, and what adds to my affliction is the shame it has brought on my family; I hope your Lordship will extend mercy to me, which will be the study of my life to shew my gratitude.

Samuel was somewhat undone by the fact that the judge stated he knew Samuel was part of a pickpocketing gang, and therefore he didn't have much sympathy. He did, however, allow Samuel to enlist in the army rather than be sent to the Australian penal colonies. Perhaps the judge had been impressed by Samuel's organisational skills, and that perhaps he may have got away with this routine many times.

The same judge may not have been so impressed by the unsophisticated approach taken by 16-year-old pickpocket Charles Brandon in the next case. His victim was having a drink with friends in the Adam and Eve public house when Charles approached him, asked him the time, and then snatched the pocket-watch before running away. When chased down, he threw away the watch, breaking it in the process.

In court he initially told the judge that it was 'just a joke', then changed his story to say that the victim was drunk so could not possibly remember what happened. Not surprisingly the judge found him guilty and he was whipped in the local gaol before being released.

Pickpocketing, of course, had been illegal long before any of the new laws brought in during the nineteenth century, so could not be the cause of any rise in juvenile crime. Also, the court records show that about three-quarters of all thefts recorded in the county of Middlesex (which contained most of London) in the first quarter of the nineteenth century were committed by people under 25 years old, the vast majority of whom were teenagers or younger boys, according to noted historian Heather Shore. Both the new legislation and the introduction of a publicly funded police force may have boosted the numbers of juveniles going to court, but it is undeniable that most courts were regularly dealing with juveniles before and after the possible 'invention' of juvenile delinquency. Not least, the courts had been dealing with pickpocketing gangs containing real-life Artful Dodgers in various large cities for a long time.

Juvenile Gangs

Pickpocketing gangs similar to Fagin's fictional gang did exist in the 1830s and 1840s (and references to them were common: see the judge's address to John Hudson in case study no. 1). However, most gangs, juvenile or otherwise, were concerned with violence, protecting their own 'patch' and enhancing their street reputation, rather than group theft. For instance, one Bradford lad remembered how it felt to be 'top of the tree' in his local neighbourhood gang:

> I'm cock a'thee. I can gob you. Cock of the turn. I'm the best fighter ... Those days if there was somebody sort of top of the tree they were always like gunfighters they'd try and get themselves a reputation ... In one fight we fought like 'Kilkenny cats'

every day from Monday till Saturday ... We fought in the mill yard at dinner time or breakfast time ...

His reminiscences have a jolly feel to them, but the problem was a serious one. In the 1850s Henry Mayhew described a frightening scene:

> Large bodies of twenty or thirty [lads], with sticks hidden down the legs of the trousers, and with these they rob and beat those who do not belong to their own gang. The gang will often consist of 100 lads, all under 20, one-fourth of whom regularly come together in a body ... they generally arrange where to meet again [to fight] on the following night.

Large violent gangs such as these certainly existed across London, but they were not just found in the capital. At the end of the nineteenth century there was a very widespread unease about the state of youth in most urban areas. Concerns centred on visible youth problems, such as drunkenness, 'loafing around on street corners' and teenage prostitution. In an attempt to avoid sexually transmitted diseases such as venereal disease, men sought out younger and younger prostitutes. The age of sexual consent was raised in 1885 from 13 to 16 in order to try to control the trade in teenage prostitutes, but the problem remained a significant one.

The violent gangs that Mayhew had talked about were still in existence as well. Labelled as 'hooligans' by the newspapers and by social commentators, they took names of their own choosing – for example, Birmingham's Peaky Blinders, Liverpool's Corner-Men and Sheffield's White Silk and Red Silk gangs (so-called because they were identified by the colour of their scarves). There were also very violent gangs operating in Scotland, with Glasgow's reputation as a 'hard city' being formed due to its large criminal gangs. Many other countries also seemed to have their own 'youth problem'. For example, in Melbourne, Australia, a group of boys known as Larrikins were involved in the rape of a 16-year-old servant girl.

Andrew Davies has researched one of the most violent gangs in England. The Manchester Scuttlers, who existed between 1880 and the 1920s, were a notorious fighting gang responsible for a number of violent fights in the late nineteenth century. Although many of the gangs were dangerous (Birmingham's Peaky Blinders, for example, earned their nickname from the face-slashings they carried out with razor-blades), the Scuttlers deserved their reputation as one of the most feared gangs in England. They committed numerous serious assaults, woundings and five murders just in their neighbourhood. One of their victims was lucky to get away with his life, or one more murder might have been added to their tally:

'The Manchester Scuttlers' – At the Manchester Police Court, a rough-looking youth named John Henry Kelly was charged with inflicting grievous bodily harm upon another youth called Joseph Wood. About nine o'clock on Thursday night, Wood and a companion were coming from Ludgate Street into Rochdale Road when they met the prisoner and others. Wood's companion stated that the prisoner rushed at Wood, and struck him on the back of the head with a poker. Wood also received a stab in the head from a large table knife. The injured youth was taken to the Royal Infirmary. (*The Clarion*, 4 June 1892)

Gang members in the 1880s and 1890s had their own 'uniforms' to identify themselves. Male gang members were resplendent in their pointed brass-tipped clogs, flared trousers, bright silk-scarves and rakishly tilted peaked caps. Their wide leather belts were decorated along their whole length with pierced hearts, serpents, clogs or animals, and perhaps the Scuttler's name or that of his girlfriend. But, as one commentator noted:

the business end of the belt was the buckle, usually a heavy brass one about three inches in diameter. A scuttle between two rival bands might well continue, on and off, for months … and the leaders of the gangs, the 'Cocks', might agree to fight it out themselves.

However, below this 'hooligan aristocracy' of the Scuttlers and the Peaky Blinders, most cities had their own smaller, less well-known, gangs; indeed individual neighbourhoods could hold a number of competing gangs of boys who fought for territory, prestige and a reputation as the toughest of the local 'mobs'. They were a constant problem for local residents (although they could also provide protection from other marauding gangs, and thus might be tolerated) and they were certainly a problem for the police:

Everyone was out on the street, to see the Black Maria, you know 'somebody's got nicked' out we come … 'God Jesus, them two lads, them two brothers have been in trouble again'. ... we'd nicked the bloody coal, aye we nicked it, well it weren't the first time we'd had it on, we went two, three bleddy times on the trot. I used to get on the coal truck, chuck the bogger [good quality coal], and my brother used to put it in the bags, too bloody heavy, the wheels on the cart fell off and the police caught us.

With the constant cat-and-mouse games played out between the police and young offenders, we could go so far as to say that the gangs and the police fought each other to maintain supremacy over the public streets. Politicians and penal reformers were undecided as to how to combat the gang problem. Some wanted to introduce harsher measures, such as the introduction of borstal in 1902, to remove gang members from the streets. Others suggested that the answer lay in better youth welfare, better housing and more opportunities for well-paid employment in order to remove the conditions which created gangs in the first place. Similar differences of opinion in how to tackle youth crime still exist today.

The Best Kind of Boy – the 'Hooligan'

While some regarded youths as a source of problems, others looked at them as a source of future promise. The well-known army officer Robert Baden-Powell, for example, expressed a preference for 'hooligans' to join his new enterprise in the early twentieth century. The Scouting movement was an attempt to channel youthful energy and vitality into more useful directions. It is likely that Baden-Powell had in mind a boisterous and impetuous child rather than a battle-hardened Scuttler when he uttered his request in 1908. However, youth movements were seen as an alternative source of 'belonging' for some young people. Scouts were taken from the cities to the countryside where they could entertain themselves in wholesome and healthy pursuits such as hiking, cycling and camping. Scouting was not a direct response to the problem of juvenile gangs (or juvenile crime for that matter). It was motivated by grave concerns over the physical fitness of volunteers for the British Army during the Boer War (1899–1902). Nevertheless, it seemed to offer a number of useful remedies for society's ills. It gave delinquent youths a useful purpose, it channelled youthful energy into healthy activities which built up the body (for the next war), and it would, it was hoped, prevent children from getting into 'mischief'.

In practice, the sort of daredevil children whose nightly adventures involved daring raids on shops, climbing over roofs, besting another gang in a fight, smoking, and impressing girls who might accompany them on their expeditions in London or Manchester's darkened streets were not interested in joining youth organisations such as the Scouts. They also had very little interest in finding employment, it seemed, or facing up to the challenges of the new century. This worried some sectors of society. The journalist and playwright George Sims lamented:

> The vital factor in the future of the British Empire is the child . . . Thousands of the tortured children who suffer and survive will only do so with stunted bodies and enfeebled minds to become the physical, moral and mental wreckage which burdens the state and fills the lunatic asylums, the workhouses, and the jails.

Sadly, the majority of the boys that Sims was talking about in 1907 would later join another institution: the British armed forces, where thousands of working-class lads filled the trenches – and died there too. One probation officer, Robert Holmes, made a study of the young people who passed through his hands and tried to find the silver lining in the mass slaughter of the First World War. Of the nearly 17,000 offenders the courts had entrusted to him, nearly 2,000 joined the armed forces in 1914. In order to remember and glorify their sacrifices, he produced a book detailing the stories of seventy-two young men who had been convicted, but subsequently joined the armed forces to fight for their country.

George was one of the boys under Holmes' charge and had been convicted of stealing food for himself and for his younger brother. They had been deserted by their parents. George became a sailor on a minesweeper when the First World War broke out, and sent regular letters home. They revealed the realities of the sacrifices made by young men like him:

> It is lonely, and I don't know how we live through the cold. I never seem to get used to the danger. I'm so frightened that I can't sleep proper. I never prayed much before, but I say many prayers now, and I should be glad if you'd pray for me now and then.

A fortnight later this letter was followed by another, this time from the captain of the ship on which George served:

> George was the only one lost, and he gave up the bit of board that would have saved him so as to let a chap have it who could not swim. He never made any shout about his pluck, and we most of us thought him a bit of a coward, but he showed us, after all, he was a game 'un, and no mistake.

George's heroic action seems to have redeemed him in the eyes of his shipmates, not to mention Holmes and, presumably, respectable society. It was a high price to pay for redemption.

Holmes' book is a reminder that young men who might be viewed as very problematic in times of peace could prove very useful in times of war. It is also a reminder of how young men were brought up to be manly, patriotic and physically strong. As a boy growing up in the early years of the twentieth century, George might have expected to fight for his country. Few boys born between 1880 and 1914 would have reached their twenty-first birthday without being encouraged to go to war in some corner of a foreign field. Masculine toughness in wartime and peacetime (within limits) was a quality to be admired. Boys did not cry if they wanted to grow up to be 'real men'. Working-class boys had a hard life that toughened them up, while middle-class boys were trained in duties that would make them officers and leaders of the working-class battalions they would command whenever the next war came about. It is easy to see how boys might have got into trouble with fighting and other kinds of masculine escapades, or when they practised being 'manly' men. The socialisation of girls seemed to produce different outcomes. How did society perceive girls and crime, and the young women who appeared to be more masculine than feminine in their behaviour and leisure activities?

Girls and Young Women

Home discipline, familial control and the impact of gendered social-ising influences kept a lot of girls out of the kinds of 'mischief' that boys got into. This kept them off the streets and out of the public eye. Oral histories can give us a glimpse of the strict upbringing and high-level of social control experienced by young women. One winter's night in 1910, while sitting in front of the fire with a group of her mother's friends, one girl let slip that she had heard that one of the neighbours was pregnant. Her mother immediately took her to the back room for a 'dressing down' for her rudeness. Good girls did not refer publicly to 'that sort of thing'. Another young woman wanted to go to a dance at a well-governed respectable dance hall:

> But my father learned of my going and stopped it immediately. I was not to dance. I think he was over-protective really and it was a fear that I might get into the wrong company and I think that he perhaps, he loved us well and therefore wished to save us from any harm that may have come but I, being young, didn't think of such things.

Parents may have had the best of intentions, but the home environment for many young women must have been oppressive and suffocating:

> My father had the greatest authority ... I think his actions, his looks, and perhaps one word or two we would know we had to behave. Not that it was necessary to do a great deal because we had been trained from an early age, the beginning you might say, to do what was correct as well as we might and he would see to it that we didn't stray from that path.

Girls and young women were strictly controlled within the home and, as those oral histories reveal, parents tried to ensure that discipline followed them out of the house as well. However, when young women were able to secure jobs (and as with working mothers, the wages earned by working daughters were often essential for the family's income) they had a certain amount of liberty which could lead them into trouble (and excitement, and love, and an increased measure of freedom as well).

Young women often left the factory or mill at the end of the day linked arm-in-arm with their workmates, and sometimes went to the pub on the way home, and sometimes they fell out with each other and got into scuffles. This brought them to the attention of the local public, as this letter to the *Nantwich Chronicle* in 1881 illustrates:

> I have the misfortune to traverse the High Street frequently in the evenings, and am sometimes foolish enough to imagine the footpath is intended for respectable persons, and not only for youths and girls to promenade; but I speedily observe my error by being jostled onto the roadway. Then in addition to this, I since heard

language uttered by young women so foul and filthy that I felt ashamed to belong to the same sex, and this is an everyday occurrence.

So, in reality, young working women were likely to act in the same way as young working men. They walked around together in large groups, and they got into arguments and fights. Some fracas also saw weapons being used, and were as brutal in character as fights between men. Witness these three examples from the 1886 *Staffordshire Advertiser*:

The court was occupied for a considerable time arising out of a number of charges arising out of a disgraceful neighbourhood quarrel in Tenterbanks on Sunday. Mary Nolan, a young woman of bad character was charged with breaking a pane of glass in a window of a house during the progress of the disturbance. The defendant's hand was cut, and the evidence was to the effect that the injury was caused by her thrusting her hand through the window. Against this the defendant alleged that her hand was cut by a knife. (9 October 1886)

Jane Lloyd was charged with assaulting her mother, who she frequently abused. 'On the day in question she struck her in the head with a poker. The complainant did not wish to press the charge, all she wanted was protection'. (14 August 1886)

Charlotte Hall was summoned for assaulting a woman leaving Messrs. Bostock's factory with her sister at one o'clock, and the defendant, who was employed at Mr Wycherley's factory, crossed the road and addressed her in very insulting language. They took no notice of the defendant, who became very excited, and caused a large crowd of operatives to follow them along the street. Opposite St Patrick's place the defendant struck her twice upon the breast with her fist. (26 February 1881)
[Charlotte was fined ten shillings but, since she was unable to come up with the money, she was sentenced to spend a month in prison.]

As these newspaper reports show, some young women committed very similar crimes to young men and because of that they ended up in prison. However, women were imprisoned in much lower numbers than young men. They committed fewer crimes in the first place, and they were less likely to be arrested when they did. Police officers considered dangerous or violently drunken men to be higher on their list of priorities than women, and certainly higher than girls. To arrest a girl invited ridicule back at the police station, and was to be avoided if at all possible. Even when the police did make an arrest, magistrates did not seem to take crimes committed by young women very seriously in the nineteenth century.

The criminal justice system, newspapers and social reformers all continued to focus firmly on young men. As we learn from Holmes' book, some male juvenile delinquents seem to have redeemed themselves with military service in the First World War (and another cohort of young men would do the same in the Second World War). But the problem of delinquency, at least in the public consciousness, had not gone away after the First World War. In fact, things had got worse. Far from carrying the world forward to a bright new twentieth-century dawn after the terrible upheavals caused by the war, many moral commentators were convinced that the seemingly dissolute and irresponsible nature of young people would hinder the country's progress as it recovered from the war years.

Into the 1920s and 1930s

Rather than marking an end to concerns about youth crime, after the First World War there were renewed concerns about delinquency. There had been a rise in crime committed by young teens during the war, and explanations for the rise of juvenile delinquency began to sound quite familiar. Commentators asked, 'Who would keep the children on the right path when their fathers had been killed during the war and their mothers were out at work trying to keep the family's head above water?' Just as society had blamed working mothers once before, so war-widows and women who did not remain at home to carry out their 'natural' child-rearing duties were in the firing line again. In 1917 The National Council of Public Morals blamed neglectful parents and also returned to the idea that youths faced over-zealous attention from the police, truancy officers and public health officials:

> There has been a tendency in recent years to increase the variety of offences with which children may be charged. For instance, children are now charged with wandering, with being without proper guardianship, with being 'beyond control'. Our streets

are now more rigidly supervised than ever before. There is a large and increasing army of officials whose duty it is to watch over child life. In many cases it has seemed to me that the zeal of those officers was not always tempered by humanity and expediency.

The cinema and popular 1930s gangster films also came in for criticism. Youths stopped pretending to be swashbuckling pirates or gun-fighting cowboys and instead started to act like American gangsters. Children appeared to find law-breakers and violence attractive. This was a trend that continued with British feature films such as *Brighton Rock* (1947), based on the 1938 Graham Greene novel, which graphically portrays violence and youth crime through the character of 'Pinkie', the juvenile leader of a vicious gang based in Brighton. Pinkie is a complex character who reflects many of the ambiguities presented by youth offenders. He had been damaged by his upbringing, he held to his own moral code which was at variance with the morality of modern respectable society, he was offered numerous opportunities to reform but seemed psychologically unable to take advantage of them, and he was capable of extreme violence and brutality. Pinkie, like many real-life young offenders, seemed to need both strong discipline and loving care; he was simultaneously a violent offender and a 'victim'. Society increasingly began to understand that children could not be separated out into 'good' and 'bad'; their characters, and the approach needed to rescue the good in all children, were much more complex than that.

With 'absent mothers', over-zealous legal authorities and popular entertainment all being blamed yet again, we can see recurring factors in many of the debates about 'juvenile delinquency'. It seems that this is a repeating pattern in British society. Geoff Pearson, in his book *Hooligan: A History of Respectable Fears*, suggested this pattern is repeated every twenty years or so. Since at least the eighteenth century, society has invented and reinvented the problem of juvenile delinquency, and then found reasons why it existed yet again. Only occasionally do we remember the experience of our history, as *The Times* did in 1964:

'Mods and Rockers in the 1880s' – Today they may be Mods or Rockers or even Teds, but there is nothing new about them, and in the last century they would have been called 'Scuttlers'. There is more than one elderly man of my acquaintance who has little good to say about the younger generation, but to whom mention of the Scuttlers brings a twinkle to the eye, and a reminiscent murmur of 'Oh aye, I remember them'.

Trying to put some of this into perspective, we have to separate out the crime that was committed by children and youths (of which there was, and still is, quite a lot) and the concept of 'juvenile delinquency'. Almost as soon as the concept of good and bad children was constructed, society began trying to identify and control children they found troublesome and problematic or who were perceived to be in need of discipline to keep them under control. Criminologists (and from the 1920s and 1930s psychologists) tried to understand the causes of juvenile delinquency, before working on strategies for punishing wrong-doers and deterring potential offenders.

There seems to be no end to our constant reinvention of juvenile delinquency. Society anxiously looked, and still looks, towards the conduct and behaviour of the young as an indication of the future. When children fail to live up to the (often unattainable) standards expected of them, we worry. What is going wrong with children? And thus a new crisis is born.

Inevitably governments try to combat any perceived rise in delinquency. The following chapter explores how new forms of punishment, which first simply treated adults and children alike, reacted to the specific challenges and needs of younger offenders by separating them from adult offenders. What did the authorities hope to achieve by this? How did the treatment of younger offenders change over time? Did the new forms of punishment make any difference?

CHAPTER THREE

DEALING WITH WAYWARD CHILDREN

From imprisonment and transportation, reformatory and industrial schools to borstals, juveniles were increasingly distinguished as having different needs from adult offenders. In the early nineteenth century, juries and prosecutors alike often recommended mercy on account of age, and *pious perjury* was often used. Pious perjury was when the value of stolen goods was deliberately undervalued by juries in criminal trials so that a less severe punishment could be imposed. This helped children to avoid the gallows. Helen Johnston found that none of the 103 under 14-year-olds who were sentenced to death at the Old Bailey between 1801 and 1836 was executed. Despite the death penalty not being abolished for all juveniles until 1908, in practice the execution of children was unusual. There were, of course, exceptions, such as the case of John 'Any Bird' Bell, a 14-year-old boy hanged for murdering another juvenile in Maidstone. Adults often had their sentences commuted (lowered) to transportation or imprisonment, but juveniles almost always did.

Early Nineteenth-Century Imprisonment

While the prison system was not organised on a national basis until 1877, the government had increasingly involved itself in the running of the prisons from the turn of the nineteenth century. In the early nineteenth century then, imprisonment simply meant confinement. Imprisonment at this time was not designed to reform; instead it was simply meant to confine the 'idle' and vagrant, debtors and those who were awaiting trial. There were exceptions but generally prisons were places to hold individuals until their punishment was decided. In these privately run, dilapidated places of confinement, juveniles would be held with adults. Indeed, juveniles as young as eight were confined to cells indiscriminately with adult offenders.

Largely as a result of campaigns run by philanthropists and humanitarians, there was a growing awareness that 'association' – the confinement of adults and children together – should stop. A select committee in 1818 found free association between prisoners in most gaols. Campaigning eventually led to the Goal Distemper Act (1774) which ordered justices to better regulate prisons, but change was slow. Due to concern over the risks of juvenile offender contamination through association, swift justice had been called for under the 1821 Bill for *The Punishment, Correction and Reform of Young Persons Charged with Privately Stealing from Houses, or the Person in Certain Cases*. While allowing juvenile offenders to be processed quickly under Summary Powers and resulting in *reduced* association during pre-trial imprisonment, it did not eliminate it. Many juveniles were still sent to local prisons, both awaiting trial and for petty offences. This often involved separate accommodation in existing prisons, but this was at the discretion of the prison governor or individual magistrates. For example, in Lancaster and Gloucester Prisons all offenders 'associated', but at Worcester the young prisoners were not only separated but also given reading and writing instruction. Sir Robert Peel (who also successfully advocated for a police force in 1829) ushered in a new classification system which separated different types of offender, but not adults and children. In 1840 there were approximately 10,000 young men in prison. The number of young offenders in English prisons fell throughout the century, but as late as 1880 there were almost 900 under 12-year-olds in gaol, and over 5,000 boys aged between 12 and 16.

The number of young people prosecuted may have risen due to the introduction of the 1847 Juvenile Offenders Act (see Chapter Two) but it caused the number of young people in prison to fall. The Act stipulated that all those under 14 years of age who committed small thefts should be tried at the magistrates' courts, and the maximum sentence was three months' imprisonment. The act further allowed for whipping to be used instead of, or in addition to, imprisonment (as in the case of Anthony Kehoe, see case study no. 12). The Juvenile Offenders Act (1850) and the Criminal Justice Act (1855) followed shortly after, which moved thefts by under 16-year-olds to the lower courts too. While sentences were short, they still resulted in the confinement of juveniles in inappropriate prisons. However, alongside imprisonment the dominant form of punishment from 1788 to 1868 was transportation 'beyond the seas'.

Transportation

By the eighteenth century, transportation as a punishment had become the routine punishment for law-breakers. As a consequence of the United States gaining independence, transportation to America was replaced with transportation to Australia in 1787. By 1868 over 130,000 men and just under 25,000 women had been transported to the Australian colonies from Britain and Ireland. The majority were sent to New South Wales and Van Diemen's Land. Transportation ended to New South Wales in 1841 and to Van Diemen's Land in 1853 but continued to Western Australia from 1850 to 1868. The British government advocated transportation as a punishment because it was seen as a deterrent and it provided cheap labour for the growing colonies. Even if it failed to deter some convicts, they would be removed from Britain and, due to the distance, were unlikely to return.

Before convicts reached the colonies, they had to be confined until a ship was ready to transport them. While females were kept in prisons, such as Millbank, males were generally confined on the hulks – decommissioned war ships converted to hold prisoners. Male juveniles sentenced to transportation often ended up in the hulks where they were locked below decks with adult offenders with little supervision. In 1816 John Capper (then Clerk for the Management of Criminal Business at the Home Office) suggested that juveniles on the hulks should be given separate accommodation. Backed up by calls from the Reverend Price, and largely thanks to Home Secretary Robert Peel, eventually most (but not all) juveniles were transferred to the juvenile-only *Bellerophon* hulk in 1822. Not only did juveniles not leave the hulks for labour, but also conditions were poor, reformation was lacking, and vice and bullying were rife, according to numerous reports. Despite the juvenile-only hulk being seen as a

HMS *Warrior* convict hulk. (Source: H. Mayhew and J. Binny, *The Criminal Prisons of London, and Scenes of Prison Life*, Vol. 3, *The Great Metropolis* (Griffin, Bohn & Company, 1862), p. 256)

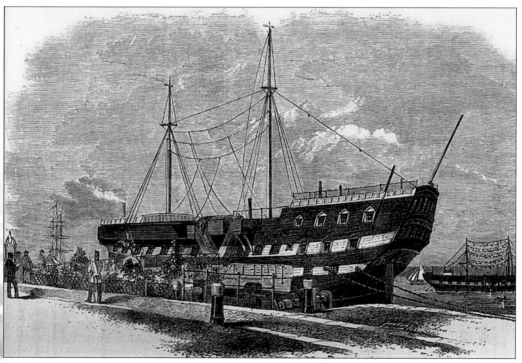

An engraving of Millbank Prison, London. Created from a photograph by Herbert Watkins. (*Wikimedia Commons*)

failure, the *Euryalus* (which replaced the *Bellerophon*) continued in use until 1843 (see case study no. 5). Moreover, practice and intentions differed and many juveniles were still confined on hulks with adult convicts.

The authorities both on the hulks and in Millbank attempted to educate their inmates. However, the matron of Millbank recorded that there was no enthusiasm for learning to read and write (Millbank had a library made up of religious works and the classics, which may not have been very appealing to the inmates). On board the hulks, female convicts received religious instruction and basic education. Elizabeth Lang Grindod's account of the *Garland Grove* voyage reported that, by the time of arrival, female convicts had taught the older children to read. Some children could read imperfectly but improved en-route, while others could read but not write and they 'gladly embraced the opportunity of learning'.

When they arrived in the penal colony, unless they were badly behaved, the convicts would be assigned to a free colonist for the purpose of carrying out work. This applied to juvenile convicts as well as adults, although young male convicts were considered to be less skilled and less physically able to undertake the work that their adult counterparts could. Consequently, they were difficult to assign;

unless they could be placed in government gangs or found work as errand boys, they were kept idle in the prisoners' barracks. Of course, there were exceptions – some boys with agricultural or commercial skills were readily employed. Despite the Molesworth Committee in 1838 pointing to a lack of reformation and the existence of sexual abuse and savage punishments, many people believed that these juveniles would be able to gain employment in the colony and re-enter society away from their criminal connections. In an attempt to deal with the difficulty of assigning juveniles to free settlers in the early days of the Port Arthur settlement (1830–1833), a number of juvenile males were sent there and instructed in trades. It was hoped that they would become both useful to the public and able to earn a reputable livelihood upon release. However, with an increasing number of juveniles financially burdening the colonial government, by 1834 a juvenile penal settlement was established at Point Puer in the Port Arthur penal establishment, Van Diemen's Land.

While the move to establish Point Puer may have been largely driven by pragmatic concerns, it also coincided with emerging ideals in Europe calling for the rehabilitation of juveniles through retraining, along with their segregation from adult criminals. It was an important step in juvenile justice, but Point Puer was only one of the experiments in training younger convicts. As early as 1803 apprenticeships for juveniles were introduced, but they were seen to be unsuccessful; also short lived was the separate training of juveniles in Carters' Barracks in Sydney, which ended in 1835. Following this, juveniles in New South Wales were assigned as apprentices straight from the ships for a period of seven years, the belief being that this long period would encourage their masters to take time to train them properly – readying them for employment after freedom. Macquarie Harbour too had its version of an apprenticeship scheme but only a limited number of juveniles benefited.

Point Puer also provided educational facilities. In the earlier period (1834–1837) instruction consisted only of plain reading, writing and basic arithmetic. Poor accommodation along with low staffing levels and deficient supplies led to practices falling short of intentions. By the 1830s the system had been widely overtaken elsewhere by the 'modern' system of education which grouped students by age and taught using the lecture method.

There were two main reports on Point Puer. The first was written by the insider Commandant Charles O'Hara Booth in 1837, and the second by Benjamin Horne, the prison inspector sent by the British government, in 1843. Booth asserted that the system used between 1834 and 1837 resulted in juveniles becoming 'proficient in the 3Rs'. Whereas Booth was happy with the system, in Horne's eyes standards were not met and his report was damning. However, Horne did assert that the trade training was superior to that provided at Parkhurst. While it had started as an open prison, by the 1840s attempts were made to restructure the settlement along the lines of segregation advocated in Britain.

Parkhurst

Shortly after the establishment of Point Puer in the colonies, reforming zeal led to the establishment of a juvenile-only prison in England in 1838. The Isle of Wight was chosen as the site to instruct juvenile offenders and ready them for the colonies. The experiment began cautiously by only taking the 'best' young offenders, who were kept separate from adult prisoners. The establishment would have a strongly disciplined environment in order to try to encourage deterrence from crime among the young. The inmates were treated harshly. Initially they were continuously shackled with iron manacles, but these were put to one side within a couple of years of Parkhurst's opening, but continuous surveillance and the silent system remained. Corporal punishment was rare but a bread and water diet was imposed for even the slightest infractions. Later, a 'Refractory Class' was introduced in which boys were kept in separate confinement and exercised by walking in silent circles and then working alone in their cells. Reading, writing and employment skills were taught and, although one critic considered it to be 'useless', the noted reformer Elizabeth Fry praised the system.

In 1839 it was decided that only juvenile convicts who were sentenced to transportation would be admitted for colonial training. It was their behaviour in Parkhurst which would decide how they would be dealt with in the colonies – whether they would arrive as free emigrants, on a conditional pardon or be confined to a government prison. In 1843 the expansion of Parkhurst enabled the *Euryalus* hulk to be closed. This development was followed by the move, in 1847, to reserve Parkhurst for juveniles over 14 years of age. Younger and more hopeful cases were sent to the Philanthropic Society for them to deal with. In this final phase Parkhurst essentially became a prison for young convicts, mirroring itself on the adult convict system; it was no longer a colonial training establishment. It also became increasingly 'penal' in nature. The 1852 Select Committee on Criminal and Destitute Children rejected Parkhurst as a model for future reformatories.

Parkhurst may have been considered a failure by contemporaries, but it established a precedent for the separate treatment of juvenile offenders in Britain.

The Female Factories

Females were dealt with differently from male convicts but *juvenile* females were not treated explicitly differently from *adult* females. They were initially assigned to free settlers to work, much like male convicts were, but usually in domestic roles. However, if no work could be found for them, or if they offended while on assignment, they would be sent to the female factories (see case study no. 2). They were called factories because they were sites of production where women were supposed to be set to work. Five female factories were established in Van Diemen's Land: Hobart Town, George Town, Cascades, Launceston and Ross. In New South Wales female factories were established in Parramatta, Bathurst, Newcastle, Port Macquarie and two in Moreton Bay. Housing only female convicts, these were places of punishment but they also housed pregnant and ill women. Female factories allowed the female convicts to be put to work but they also served as places of reception and hiring when increasing numbers of females arrived. Like the male convicts, the females were 'ideally' classified according to behaviour. However, overcrowding largely hampered the system. The hard labour that the women were required to carry out included spinning, carding, washing and picking cloth. The experience varied according to the period when the women were confined, and the factory they were in. In the larger factories there was a wider range of work available, including spinning, straw plaiting, factory duties, housekeeping, working in the hospital, sewing, laundry and weaving. Badly behaved female convicts or repeat offenders were set to breaking rocks and picking oakum (a particularly unpleasant task which involved unravelling tar-coated naval ropes that cut the hands of the poor people punished in this way for their offences 'under sentence'). Offences included being drunk and disorderly, falling pregnant while on assignment, and prostitution, and more serious crimes such as theft and assault. Sentences in the factory ranged from fourteen days to a number of years. While they were primarily envisaged as places of labour, this was not always the case due to a lack of resources and overcrowding. For example, Hobart Town Female Factory, established in 1822, lacked hard labour because it was short of equipment and space to work.

The prevailing views about femininity meant that some punishments that men endured were not thought suitable for women. While conditions in the female factories were often poor, female convicts did not experience chain-gangs or flogging. Punishments which were previously used on women, including head shaving, iron collars and the stocks, were phased out. Instead, female factories were the mainstay of female punishment. The 'difficulties in finding suitable punishments for female offenders', as one magistrate explained, eased over time as more infrastructure was built – but these too became overcrowded. The system was not considered as brutal as the regimes for male convicts, but conditions were still poor and strict. The 1841–1843 *Inquiry into Female Convicts' Discipline* highlighted the overcrowding, poor nutrition and lack of separation between classes, not to mention corrupt officers. A 'strict regimen of silence and task work' was introduced (the original report is held at the Tasmanian Archives and Heritage Office Archives in the State Library of Tasmania, CSO/22/1/50, but has been transcribed by Lucy Frost and Sally Rackham, and can be downloaded at https://www.femaleconvicts. org.au/docs/disciplineinquiry/TranscriptofInquirywithtables.pdf). Despite this enforced discipline, or perhaps because of it, the female factories such as Cascades became notorious for riots as the female inmates resisted the oppressive rules. As well as female factories, the *Anson*, a hulk moored on the River Derwent, was used to house new arrivals in Van Diemen's Land from 1843 to 1847 and to train them in domestic service for six months. The constant changes in the system of governing, managing and training convicts meant that some young female convicts never spent any time at these institutions, while others spent a large proportion of their sentence at one or a number of these factories.

Reformatory and Industrial Schools

Following ideas developed by the Philanthropic Society in the late eighteenth century, one of the first reformatories was established at the Stretton Colony in Warwickshire in 1818. An early agency for female offenders, known as the 'School of Discipline' in Chelsea, was founded in 1825 and was later certified as a reformatory. These were voluntary institutions operated in the main by faith organisations. A philanthropic venture in the early nineteenth century, which became known as the 'Children's Friends Society' (more formally the Society for the Suppression of Juvenile Vagrancy), was founded by Captain Edward Pelham Brenton. The Society housed and trained juveniles for three to six months and then often indentured them as apprentices abroad in places such as the Cape in South Africa. Brenton would not take criminal youths, but instead aimed to prevent the children of the impoverished working classes from *becoming* criminal. The society was short lived, running from 1830 to 1839. The transportation of youths had taken place long before Benton's venture but he introduced the idea of providing suitable training for future colonial service. Partly due to such child-orientated schemes, there was a growing awareness that children deserved separate treatment within the justice system itself. Aftercare institutions were initially not officially part of the criminal justice system but their ideas and practices fed into the discourse surrounding juvenile offenders, and certainly influenced the establishment of the concept of *diversion*. For example, the Philanthropic Society sought to reform and reintegrate criminal juveniles. Formed by Robert Young, the Society sought to create a 'superior class of mechanics' but it was not until 1816 that Young's ideas were revisited, and Sir John Eardley-Wilmot collected funds to establish an 'after-care asylum'. These institutions were not established to replace prisons but to provide progressive establishments which later influenced how juvenile offenders were treated.

The reformatories and industrial schools eventually established in England were influenced by European practices. The French agricultural reform school at Mettray was held up as a splendid example of reform by men such as the Reverend Sydney Turner (founder of the Philanthropic Society) and the reformer Matthew Davenport Hill. It was the establishment of Mettray in France in 1839 which pulled in travelling philanthropists from the Netherlands, Germany and England. These visits led to the formation of similar establishments in Europe, including Red Hill. Mettray was an icon of reformatory education, but so too was Germany's Rauhes Haus, established in 1833. The first to adopt a 'family' organization, it recruited religiously motivated staff and it led the farm school movement. But by the 1850s Mettray was considered the example to follow. There, boys lived in huts as family units and responded to moral influences and an elaborate rewards system, instead of severe punishment. It was thanks to a visit to Mettray in the 1840s that Turner recommended, with the support of the government, taking juvenile prisoners from London into Red Hill. For the first time the criminal justice system was explicitly linked to the reformatory schools. As Red Hill grew, it moved to St George's-in-the-Fields, and started to accommodate the children of offenders (initially both sexes) and juvenile offenders. The reception of girls ended in 1849 when the school was relocated to Red Hill. In order to mobilise public opinion, reformatory activists organised conferences on 'Preventative and Reformatory Schools' and 'Juvenile Delinquency'.

In 1852 a committee of the House of Commons was appointed to examine the treatment of criminal and destitute children, and how to implement industrial and reformatory training. Later, a series of parliamentary committees resulted in the first Reformatory Schools Act (1854), which enabled the courts to commit offenders under 16 years of age to a reformatory for not less than two years and not more than five. However, reformation would only follow fourteen days in prison. It was not until 1899 that children could be sent directly to the reformatory without going to prison first.

The reformatory regime followed a strict routine of six hours' industrial training, three hours' schooling and two hours' exercise and recreation, with the rest of the time spent at meals and on household chores. A heavily regimented routine remained the main feature and was applied especially on the school ships. School ships, such as the *Akbar* in Cheshire, were former naval ships moored to accommodate juveniles for reformation. The goal, as pointed out by Sydney Turner, was not to teach specific skills but to impart the habits of industry for employment on release. In reality, these schools often resorted to menial, but profitable, occupations for boys. For females, Mary Carpenter established a similar routine at the female schools of Red Lodge and Park Row, on the basis of restoring not only the discipline, restraint and obedience that she felt were incumbent on childhood, but also the passivity of girlhood. While males were readied for hard and independent work, the females were prepared for domestic life. Nevertheless, Carpenter stressed that female domestic training should not be at the expense of formal education. In reality, for females this meant that few gained any experience with sewing machines and other labour-saving devices. Instead, most were confined to the monotonous duties of maids and seamstresses, and carrying out domestic chores for the establishment. As historian Margaret May has pointed out, secular education was often impeded by industrial training. There was also a system of rewards and punishments. Juveniles were assessed according to general conduct, industry and overall performance. Privileges or penalties were attached to each grade, and this in turn was linked to their discharge. Arrivals were placed in the lowest grade and promoted based on favourable behavioural reports. Those in the highest grade would receive privileges including dietary rewards and extra responsibilities. A trust system was implemented in many of the institutions, in line with practices at Mettray, and invariably included greater freedom. The greatest freedom test of all came when they were discharged from the reformatory or industrial school. For the duration of their licence period they were expected to undertake honest employment.

The reformatories remained under voluntary management, but were given legal powers to detain and control juveniles in their care, and Treasury contributions were authorised. Reformatories also had to be certified by the Secretary of State and inspected by an Inspector of Prisons. Of course, magistrates did not *have* to send juveniles to reformatories and so initially they were slow in doing so. Juveniles were still sent to prison, but the tide was turning. The Act of 1857 enabled local authorities to contribute to the establishment of reformatories, and juveniles were now released on conditional licence when they had served at least half of their sentence.

The same year, industrial schools were placed in a national legal setting (amended by later Acts in 1860, 1861 and 1866). Industrial schools were established as primarily training schools for non-criminal but morally endangered children under 14 years of age. It was also initially believed that removing a child from neglectful or criminal parents to an area well away from their criminal connections would aid reformation. Under the 1861 Act, children under 14 years of age could be sent to an industrial school if they were found begging or receiving alms, were found vagrant or in the company of reputed thieves, or if their parents could not control them; children under 12 years of age could be sent to an industrial school if they had committed an offence punishable by imprisonment. Unlike reformatory placement, no preliminary period of imprisonment was required. Industrial schools were similar to reformatories; they also gained Treasury contributions, were controlled by the Secretary of State, and had to be inspected. The Inspector of Reformatories, with Assistant Inspectors, eventually became the Inspector of Reformatories and Industrial Schools. Local authorities were also, in 1872, empowered to establish these schools. The scope of the schools was extended by the Elementary Education Acts of 1870 and 1876 which empowered justices to send children to industrial schools for truancy. Apart from limiting industrial work to four hours because of their youth, industrial schools followed the same routine, but the extra time was generally devoted to household work rather than extra education. The use of such institutions meant that many, but not all, juveniles were kept out of prison. It was not until the Prison Act (1865) that those under 16 years of age had to be kept separate and were given special treatment in prison.

Because juveniles were still being confined (albeit for short periods), the Howard Association (which still advocates today for penal reform) called for an end to the imprisonment of young children. William Harcourt, as Home Secretary, sent a circular to magistrates requesting consideration of alternatives to imprisonment. Despite

Offerton Industrial School, Greater Manchester, England (1902). *(Wikimedia Commons)*

proposals made at the Eighth Conference of Discharged Prisoners Aid Societies in 1893, and by the Gladstone Committee the following year, the imprisonment of juveniles was not abolished. Finally, after almost universal condemnation of the practice by those involved in the penal system, in 1901 judges drew up a schedule of 'Normal Punishments' for juveniles under 16 years of age. It was stated that 'those under 16 years of age and convicted of property offences, without violence, would no longer be imprisoned'. The situation did not immediately change, but there were improvements. In 1905 the first juvenile court was established in Birmingham. By 1910 only 143 juveniles (i.e. under 16 years of age) were in prison.

Borstal

The founder of the best-known and most often-referenced juvenile institution – the borstal – was Sir Evelyn Ruggles-Rise. The fundamental founding principles were strict classification, firm and exact discipline, hard work and organised supervision on discharge. These institutions were established with austere discipline and while this disciplinary aspect remained, over time the training focus became much more educational in character. Trade training and basic education had been the founding principles but then came the abolishment of uniforms, and staff recruited from public schools and universities as housemasters. The 'house system' was implemented and the housemasters were to oversee the education but also maintain close personal contact with the inmates.

The borstal scheme was established as an experiment in 1900 for young offenders aged from 16 to 21. This age group was seen as being too old for reformatory training but too young to be sent to prisons, where they were at risk of being corrupted by incorrigible adult offenders. These juvenile-adults were viewed as eligible for special treatment because they had 'undeveloped characters', as had been evidenced in W.D. Morrison's *Juvenile Offenders* (1896). Initially only eight boys were selected for the experiment; they were sent to Bedford prison and kept separate from the rest of the prison population. In 1907 a bill was introduced to Parliament, with no voices of dissent, and under the Prevention of Crimes Act (1908) borstal became a separate and legally recognised part of the penal system. This Act laid down the conditions under which borstal treatment could be ordered. It explicitly stated that the offender had to have criminal habits, tendencies or associations with persons of bad character, and juvenile-adults with previous good character were excluded. Modifications were introduced in the Criminal Justice Acts of 1914 and 1925.

The criteria for admittance were that an offender must be aged between 16 and 21 and convicted on indictment by assizes or quarter sessions (today we would call this the Crown Court) for an offence punishable by imprisonment or penal servitude; in addition, they must possess criminal habits or tendencies, or habitually mix with persons of bad character. They could then be sent to a borstal. In a magistrates' court there was an additional hurdle: it was also necessary to prove that the offender had a previous conviction or had previously been discharged on probation.

A borstal sentence was for a minimum of two or three years, with the possibility of early release on licence, followed by a period of supervision. Magistrates' courts could only recommend borstal training when committing a defendant to a higher court because their sentencing powers were insufficient, and could only directly send someone to borstal if they had absconded from an approved school. While the Criminal Justice Act (1948) raised the upper age to 23, the change was unsuccessful and it was quickly reversed. The Act also changed the length of training. The full length was established as three years and a minimum detention period of nine months was introduced (previously three months for females and six months for males). By the 1930s borstals were a well-respected institution. Education, trade training and developing a sense of responsibility were the guiding principles. With low re-conviction rates in 1939, the borstal system was viewed as a success. At this time, it was believed that the borstal system would reform future adult offenders and therefore fewer prisons would be needed going forward.

The change in direction of the borstal system away from open institutions and education towards increased penal ties had begun with the problems arising during the war. In 1939 two-thirds of the borstal population had been discharged, and five institutions were closed. The increase in post-war crime led to increased borstal committals but accommodation was lacking. Escapes had always been a part of the borstal system but they had increased, throwing into question the use of open institutions. New open institutions *had* been opened, including Gaynes Hall, Huntercombe, Hewell Grange and Gringley Camp. Essentially, what had before the war been an experiment for a small group of select boys became a substantial part of the system by 1946 and it was assumed that the increase in absconders was due to an increase in open institutions. By the 1950s the borstal system was regarded as a failure and detention centres were being used as an alternative to long-term borstal training.

Open borstals for boys and girls had been established to teach their inmates to value the freedom they had been given, so that they would not abuse their freedom when they were eventually released. While there was still routine and structure, inmates were either kept in open dormitories (i.e., at Lowdham, North Sea Camp and Hollesley Bay Colony) or in closed institutions (i.e., Rochester, Portland, Feltham, Camp Hill and Sherwood). Each institution operated a different regime. Reception centres (Wormwood Scrubs and later Latchmere House) were used to ensure proper allocation to these establishments. North Sea Camp housed males who were engaged in reclaiming the land from the sea. It was windswept and endured a harsh climate in the winter. The work was rigorous and hard but the staff shared the same hardships. Hewell Grange was for the youngest and best-behaved juveniles, whereas Sherwood was for those aged 20 and 21 with bad records.

Trade training was always an intended part of the borstal system but practice fell short of intention. After the war vocational training did expand when Ministry of Labour and National Service courses became available at all borstals. A higher proportion of boys had more constructive work to do. The Advisory Council agreed that trade training was an important factor in developing character but saw its actual practical value as limited since only 30 per cent who passed through followed the trade on discharge. Moreover, the majority of boys carried out simple labour and farm jobs. By 1874 only a minority benefited from trade training.

As well as trade training and education, another feature of the borstal was its after-care programme. The Gladstone Committee's early recommendations added that 'special arrangements ought to be made for receiving and helping the inmates on discharge'. While after-care was made statutory in the 1908 Act, no specific society was authorised to carry out the work. Nevertheless, from 1911 onwards the number of associates grew and help was enlisted from organisations such as the Church of England Temperance Society, the Society of Friends and the Missions to Seamen in the ports. An arrangement was also made with police allowing these juvenile-adults to get help if they found themselves without resources. However, in reality, although after-care associates were encouraged to establish a relationship with their charges, visits were infrequent. It was acknowledged that permanent staff would be necessary for after-care to be successful but few areas had a sufficiently high concentration of these juvenile-adults to justify establishing dedicated centres – except Liverpool, where one opened in 1929, and London, where they were supervised by Borstal After-Care's permanent staff of social case-workers. By 1932 the probation officers accepted in principle being officially responsible for this after-care, but it was only in 1948 that after-care became a statutory responsibility. Under the Criminal Justice Act (1948) the newly formed Central After-Care Association coordinated all after-care work.

The number of females committed to borstal was always far smaller than the number of males, as was the case with adult offenders. There were 151 females compared with 2,109 males in borstals in 1946. Occupation for females within the borstal was generally domestic work with little effort being given to other areas, as pointed out in *The Howard League of Penal Reform* study by Elkin and Kittermaster.

After-care for females, as with males, involved finding employment as soon as possible after discharge in cooperation with the Ministry of Labour and National Service. The majority of these females were found work in factories, mills, canteens, or hospitals as ward maids and ward orderlies, or as cooks or waitresses. Some were sent into private domestic work or to farms. While many wished to join the women's services or go into nursery nursing, this proved difficult until they gained a reference first. The war years led to an increase in the number of females committed to borstal, and in order to cope with the influx the female wings at Durham Prison and Exeter Prison were both turned into female borstal institutions. The reception centre for female juvenile-adults was in Holloway Prison, where complete segregation from adults was not always possible. East Sutton Park opened in 1946 as the first open institution for girls, where they worked as part of the local rural community.

The proposals in the government White Paper 'Penal Practice in a Changing Society' (1959) and in the Advisory Council on the Treatment of Offenders' Report on the 'Treatment of Young Offenders' (1959) reflected a changing attitude towards the treatment of young offenders. The ideal of keeping young offenders out of prison was maintained, but the proposals were more penal in character. The Criminal Justice Act (1961) combined the borstal system with the

Hewell Grange Borstal. *(Wikimedia Commons)*

prisons for young offenders to become 'custodial training'. More *closed* institutions were called for, and open institutions would not be expanded. The 1961 Act ensured that short-term imprisonment was replaced with detention centres. It was becoming harder and harder to distinguish between borstals and prisons. In 1982 the Criminal Justice Act finally abolished the borstal system, replacing them with youth custody centres.

Changing views about the best way to punish young offenders, to deter other children from getting into trouble, and to reform those who were able to leave crime behind (especially through education and the provision of employment skills) meant that children experienced many different 'regimes' over the course of the last two centuries. A child who stole a few items could be sent to Australia in the 1800s, imprisoned in Parkhurst in the 1850s, sent to a reformatory in the 1870s, or kept in a borstal after 1908 – all for the same crime. Politicians and reformers argued about which types of punishment were most effective. Similar arguments persist to the present day. By looking at the impact of different punishments we might be able to see how transportation or imprisonment affected the whole lives of people who were convicted as children. How, though, do we find out enough information on these children?

49

CHAPTER FOUR

RESEARCHING CHILDREN'S LIVES

So far in this book we have discussed how the criminal justice system dealt with 'troublesome' children, and in the following chapter we will see how the children coped with what they might have seen as a 'troublesome' criminal justice system. Throughout we have used criminal records to explore children's lives within the system, and sometimes looking at what their lives were like outside the prisons and reformatories in which they were confined. We know more about the people who got into trouble, often because the records created to document their time under sentence are so full of information. It is ironic that we know so much less about the law-abiding. Non-elite lives are so difficult to uncover, especially juveniles.

There are many nineteenth- and twentieth-century criminal justice sources available for reference, but they are not without their own unique problems. They were generated originally by organisations whose motive was to punish and reform criminals, and were shaped by the needs of the particular institution for which they were written. Despite these limitations, tracing juveniles from one record to another still allows us to understand the progress people made in their lives. This enables a much more rounded picture of juvenile offenders to be created.

Records which document juveniles' interactions with the justice system are widely spread, so it can be a difficult and time-consuming task to trace young offenders. However, the Digital Panopticon project (www.digitalpanopticon.org) has linked together disparate social and legal records allowing the reconstruction of the juvenile offenders' lives so that researchers can follow individuals from the courtroom to their place of punishment and beyond to reveal their familial, occupational and social lives. The website allows us to search millions of separate records relating to the lives of 90,000 convicts sentenced at the Old Bailey, to research individual convict life-archives, and to learn more about crime and criminal justice more broadly. While London is the hub of this resource, there is a multitude of records relating to offenders from all of Britain. This digital repository allows users to search for individuals across multiple datasets and to 'zoom in' on particular documents that add detail to life histories. It is possible to uncover the health of juvenile offenders and whether it was affected by their punishment. The rest of this chapter describes some of the more important and informative records used in tracing the lives of young offenders in the nineteenth and twentieth centuries.

Juveniles on Trial

The Old Bailey, which is the Central Criminal Court in London, produced trial records that have now been digitised. For over 240 years trial reports were published at the conclusion of every session of the court, and together they now form the largest body of texts detailing non-elite lives ever published. All surviving records, from 1674 to 1913, are freely available on the Old Bailey Online website (www.oldbaileyonline.org), containing images of the original pages of the proceedings, with key word and criteria searchable text. As well as details of the crime and sentence, certain demographic information and rich witness and offender testimonies are available in the online repository, which includes nearly 200,000 trials. The Old Bailey proceedings are useful but they are not without their limitations, and it is important to consider why it was published and who had access to it. Trial records are official texts and they construct accounts of behaviour according to the values of the period in which they were written. Yet, a trial is one of the rare moments in which

Thomas Rowlandson and Augustus Pugin [1808], 'The Old Bailey' in Rudolph Ackermann, William Henry Pyne and William Combe (eds), *The Microcosm of London or, London in Miniature*, vol. 2 (London, 1904).

detailed information is recorded on the working classes and their children. Through these trial records it is possible to uncover the types and number of crimes committed by young people, and how they were treated in court.

Yet it must be born in mind that these court records do not record every single word spoken during the trial. They were edited by the clerk and reflect what he thought was important enough to record for posterity. It must also be remembered that the Central Criminal Court only dealt with the more serious crimes. Consequently, we know much less about the petty crimes committed by young people, that were dealt with by magistrates in local courts rather than by Judges in London (see Chapters Two and Three).

Transported Young Convicts

The widespread stigmatisation of Australia's convict past resulted in some documentation not being preserved. Thankfully, however, while many records were destroyed or disappeared, many convict records have survived (some for New South Wales and many for Van Diemen's Land and Western Australia). The *New South Wales State Archives and Records* preserved a range of convict records from which the lives of convict juveniles can be uncovered. These include: the early *Convict Indents* (or Convict Indentures) which are official lists of convicts transported on board particular ships; *Certificates of Freedom* which were awarded at the completion of the convicts' sentence; and *Tickets of Leave* which were awarded for good conduct. While the regulations of the conditional early release scheme under Tickets of Leave changed over time, they essentially allowed convicts to live on their own account within certain restrictions (including geographical restrictions).

Conditional and *Absolute Pardons* were awarded for good conduct but conditional pardons were usually awarded with the proviso that they did not return to the country of their conviction. Lastly, convicts had to apply for permission to marry; permission could be refused on the grounds of bad conduct or an existing marriage, so officials kept records of this process which can be useful to researchers. While available documentation does cover the whole period of convict transportation to New South Wales, the amount of information available varies within different periods and for different individuals. Moreover, there is little information of the convicts' life under sentence (such as their employment assignments and their conduct).

Nevertheless, it is possible to trace juvenile convicts from the courts in Britain to their punishment in New South Wales. Then, depending on the period, other types of documentation can be used in order to fill in the details, such as online digitised newspapers.

When researching offenders, it is rarely possible to rely on a single resource. However, the Digital Panopticon is a great place to start. Information about convicts transported to Van Diemen's Land has been pulled together from *VDL Founders and Survivors Convicts 1802–1853* and the *Tasmanian Archives and Heritage Office*, and linked to other digitised datasets. The types of record available for convicts sent to Van Diemen's Land include, but are not limited to:

- *Muster Records* these provide information on the changing locations of the convict and their assignments;
- *Appropriation Records* these state each convict's trade and how their skill was used; often included is the name of the settler to whom the convict was assigned, or the government department responsible for the convict;
- *Conduct Records* these provide information on the offenders' behaviour in the colony; offences, punishments and locations were recorded, along with the date. Initiated by Lieutenant-Governor Arthur, these ran from 1803 and recorded the convict's offences from their arrival, and details of their previous convictions and behaviour prior to embarkation. These records inform us of the offenders' status: whether they were assigned or whether they were stationed or confined, for example, on public works or in a penal station such as Port Arthur; and
- *The Description List* created to keep track of convicts, this provides enough information to enable us to create a basic sketch of what the offender looked like, including tattoos and height information – humanising the juvenile offender in question. Information on their trade and birth place is also often included. George Fenby's record, for example, tells us that the 10-year-old 'tailor boy' had fair hair, an oval face and was from Shadwell Parish, London.

The system of convict transportation and the detailed bureaucratic records on individual offenders which the system created allow us to recreate the experiences of young people during and after convict detention in the colony. Essentially, until a convict received a pardon

NAME *Geo. Fenby* No. *410*

Trade *Tailor boy*

Height *without Shoes* *4/0½*

Age *10.*

Complexion *fair*

Head *round*

Hair *brown*

Whiskers *none*

Visage *oval*

Forehead *ppendic*

Eyebrows *bro*

Eyes *d brown*

Nose *Short*

Mouth *m w*

Chin *M L.*

Remarks *none*

George Fenby's Description List (CON18–1–15) (Available at LINC).

or free certificate, he remained in what was *effectively* a prison without walls, resulting in a huge amount of invaluable biographical and life-course material for research. Using a combination of these records it is therefore possible to trace the progress of hundreds and thousands of young people who were forcibly emigrated to Australia. But what happened to those who were sentenced to spend their time in British prisons? How can we research their experiences?

Confined Juveniles

Prison records relating to individual prisoners are held in a number of different places including The National Archives in London, county and city record offices, and, occasionally, the prisons themselves. The local archives are a good starting point. Juveniles were confined in local prisons alongside adults and serious offenders well into the nineteenth century and it is possible to search for juvenile offenders in, for example, the Newgate Prison Calendars. Similarly, hulk and prison registers can also be used. Specifically, the Prison Registers (Millbank, Parkhurst, Pentonville) 1847–1866 and Register of Prisoners in County Prisons 1838–1875 give each prisoner's age, certain familial information, their literacy level, trade, trial and conviction details, sentence, previous convictions, and movements within the prison system.

Not all of these registers are available online (although some can be viewed at Find My Past) but they are freely available at *The National*

Archives. Moreover, it is possible to trace juvenile offenders who continued to offend as adults in the *UK Licences for the Parole of Convicts 1853–1925*. These documents contain detailed information on offences (including those that people committed in their youth), punishments, demographic information, family life, occupations, literacy, behaviour and health in prison. *The Home Office and Prison Commission Licences for the Parole* (known by their collection names PCOM 3 and PCOM 4) are available for both male and female convicts. From 1853 onwards the Penal Servitude Act allowed the release of offenders serving time in convict prisons on a 'conditional licence' before their sentence was finished (much like the tickets of leave and pardons used in Australia, see above). While licence details vary, they generally include details of conviction, release date and licence conditions. They may also include previous convictions, marital status, children, next of kin, addresses, associates and visitors, prison labour details, conduct, medical information and even personal correspondence (when convicts wrote letters to people the prisons thought were unsuitable because they had criminal convictions or were known prostitutes, the letters were not sent but kept on file). As we have already discovered in Chapter Three, most young people who committed an offence, or who were considered 'at risk' of doing so, were never sent to prison. Instead they were 'diverted' into industrial or reformatory schools.

Children in Reformatory and Industrial Schools and Young Adults in Borstal

Reformatory, industrial and borstal records are not digitised but it is still possible to explore the physical documents they created at the archives (particularly but not exclusively the London Metropolitan Archives (LMA) and The National Archives). For example, the records of Her Majesty's Young Offender Institute and Remand Centre, Feltham (archive code LMA/4465) are available at the LMA. Feltham is an interesting place to study.

The Middlesex Industrial School opened in Feltham in 1859 and did not close until 1909. The premises then came under the control of the Prison Commissioners and Feltham Borstal Institution opened in 1910 (see Chapter Three). In 1939 Feltham absorbed prisoners from the Boys' Prison at Wormwood Scrubs. This included boys awaiting trial, prisoners and those awaiting allocation to a borstal (such as the

Wormwood Scrubs Prison entrance. (*Wikimedia Commons*)

last case study, Brendan Behan; see also Chapter Three). In 1942 the remand centre moved back to Wormwood Scrubs but the Borstal Reception Centre and the Boys' Prison remained at Feltham. In early 1945 the reception centre also went back to Wormwood Scrubs. By 1946 the Boys' Prison at Feltham had ceased to exist and Feltham reverted to being solely a borstal. In the early 1970s it was recognised that the buildings were inadequate, leading to the new Feltham opening in 1983. HM Young Offender Institution and Remand Centre Feltham was formed through the amalgamation of Ashford Remand Centre and Feltham Borstal in 1991. For this evolving institution records available at the LMA include *Governor's Journals 1910–1951* and the *History of Feltham Industrial School*, both of which allow us to learn about the establishment's rich history and how it was run. Also available are *Records of Inmates*, which enables us to carry out research on the individuals who spent time within the institution (these records include the *Nominal registers 1922, 1927–1969, Indexes to registers 1932–1969, Nominal registers for Boys' Prison at Wandsworth 1924–1939*, and *Feltham 1939–1946*. It must be noted that since some of these institutions were still in use well into the late twentieth century, access to records of people imprisoned as youths may be restricted. Usually records that contain personal information about

59

young prisoners are closed for seventy-five years. It is worth contacting the archives before visiting to ensure that the records exist and are available to view.

Criminal Petitions

The Criminal Petitions are a very detailed source but are only available for 16,309 people for the period between 1817 and 1858. They provide information on the family unit, economy and general background of the offender, as well as recording the pains of separation between parents and their convicted children. Convicted criminals, or their family and friends, made a petition when they wanted to have a sentence revoked or reduced. In the case of juvenile offenders' petitions were generally written by their parents although they were sometimes written by more literate acquaintances on the parents' behalf. Such records often reflect the bonds within the family. Criminal Petitions are available at The National Archives but many are also digitised on Find My Past.

Criminal records were, unfortunately for researchers, written from the perspective of the authorities, and were never meant for public consumption. While criminal records are invaluable, they also leave a number of gaps in our knowledge about the lives of young people. We know most about the time they spent inside an institution, but this is usually only a small part of their lives. Some of those gaps can be partially filled, however, by turning to non-criminal records including newspapers, and birth, death and marriage records.

Non-Criminal Records

Because the criminal records are *so* good, researchers become accustomed to seeing the children we are studying as offenders, living the lives of prisoners, convicts or reformatory scholars. But, for the vast majority of people, offending was an episode, a blip in their lives. It was something that they grew out of when they reached adulthood. They held down jobs, found partners and had children. They put their criminal past behind them, and we should remember to place their offending within a proper perspective. So how can looking at non-criminal records help us to do this? How can they help to fill in the gaps?

As well as newspapers, we are fortunate to also have census records and birth, marriage and death records available to us. *Census* returns available for England and Wales run between 1841 and 1911.

Using the census, it is possible to find a juvenile offender's location, type of residence, family structure and occupation. Also useful are *Parish Records* of births, marriages and deaths. Together, these provide information on the individual's location, family size, child mortality and length of life. However, not all parish records have survived and they were not uniformly kept. It was not until 1836 that Parliament passed an Act for Registering Births, Deaths and Marriages in England in order to make up for the inefficiencies of parish registers. This was closely followed by a registration act passed in Van Diemen's Land in 1838, the first British colony to do so. No records are without their flaws, however. Every birth, marriage and death within the free population of the colony was supposed to be included, but many names were omitted, so it should not be taken as wholly reliable.

Census records are comparatively easy to obtain and easy to use – though you may need deep pockets to access online census records. *Parish records* are harder to access, though, again, many are now available on a pay-per-view basis. They are also much harder to read – a magnifying glass and a lot of patience will be required for some registers, particularly the earlier ones.

Newspapers

Newspaper trial reports may provide background information on offenders' lives, such as their families and occupations. Furthermore, newspapers can tell us something about how events were viewed by society. Invaluable digitised newspaper archives include *19th Century Newspapers Online*, *The Times Digital Archive*, *The British Newspaper Archive* and *Trove*. In the nineteenth century newspapers discovered that their readers liked human interest stories and consequently they printed more trial reports, complete with details of each case, with witness statements, 'witty' comments made by solicitors and judges, and the names of defendants. Newspapers sensationalised crime, and only reported criminal events they deemed 'newsworthy'. Still, they are essential for providing details about offenders and offences which cannot be found in any other sources. They can also confirm findings from other documents which may be difficult to decipher due to difficult handwriting or poor-quality preservation.

It is possible to find notices placed in the papers by relatives. See, for example, the newspaper notice for juvenile convict George Fenby, placed by his mother, Hannah Timms.

NOTICE.

IF GEORGE FENBY, who was some time back employed in the district of the Wimmera, will apply in Geelong he will much oblige his mother, Hanna Timms.

Geelong,
August 9, 1850.

Geelong Advertiser, 10 August 1850.
(*Available on Trove*)

ATTEMPT AT HIGHWAY ROBBERY.—An examination took place at the police office, yesterday, before the Police Magistrate, on a charge of attempt at highway robbery, on the Bridgewater road, upon Norman M'Kinnon and Robert Kibble, who appeared at the office to prosecute George Fenby, alias Timms, and William M'Cormick. George Fenby, it will be recollected, and another man named Timms, also implicated in this charge, but not yet apprehended, were about a year ago fully committed from the police office at Portland on a similar charge, and who upon their trial before the Resident Judge of the Supreme Court, in Melbourne, obtained a verdict in their favor and were discharged. The case of Fenby and M'Cormick was gone into at some length yesterday, and they both were remanded for further evidence until 10 o'clock this day.

Portland Guardian and Normanby General Advertiser, Local News, 27/08/1842.
(*Available on Trove*)

Before her marriage in the colonies, Hannah (aka Hanna) Timms was known as Hannah Fenby. Both Hannah and George were convicted of theft together at the Old Bailey but they were transported on separate ships to Van Diemen's Land. This article evidences how Hannah, now a remarried and free woman, reached out to her child.

Another, earlier, newspaper article featuring George shows that not only was his offending career not over, but also that he may have spent time with his mother in the colonies as he adopted her new surname 'Timms'. As can be seen from these examples, it is possible to find information about offenders that is not related to their crimes but is critical for a wider understanding of their lives and experiences.

Another, more specialist, newspaper is the *Police Gazette*, originally called *Hue and Cry*, which was circulated to police stations with details of people the police wished to interview; these contain detailed physical descriptions of individual men and women. Essentially the *Police Gazette* was issued by the police to help fight crime. It contains information on wanted criminals, crimes committed, criminals who had been apprehended, and missing persons. Therefore, information which can be uncovered includes name of criminal, birth year, crime, location, role in crime and conviction place. The *Gazette* invited the public to report crimes and to offer rewards for information leading to conviction. It is unknown how effective the *Gazette* was in tackling crime, but it was widely read. It also carried details of stolen property and wanted people. Wood engravings of stolen valuables, photographs of criminals and a classified system of descriptions became features of the publication under Sir Howard Vincent (first director of the Criminal Investigation Division). The original *Gazette* was founded in 1772 by John Fielding (chief magistrate of the Bow Street Police Court). The name was changed to the *Police Gazette* in 1828, and responsibility for the publication was transferred to Scotland Yard in 1883.

Copies of the *Police Gazette* are available at several locations including the British Newspaper Archive, which has a digital repository with 739 issues for the following dates: 1773–1776, 1829, 1858, 1880, 1898 and 1916–1918. Ancestry's archive has copies from the periods 1812–1902 and 1921–1927. They are also available at the National Archives (HO 75) and the British Library.

Non-Criminal Institutions

While certainly not all criminal children were orphans, we would be remiss if we did not outline some of the institutions in which destitute children, or children otherwise in need, could be kept. As this book is about children who have been caught up the criminal justice system there is only room here to mention a few of these institutions. The care of destitute children was largely left to charities. One of the earliest orphanages was the Foundling Hospital founded by Thomas Coram in 1741, which attempted to look after infants whose parents had abandoned them or could not care for them. Surviving records of charities are largely kept by local record offices, although not all have survived. Searching 'Discovery' (the digital repository) on the National Archives website, or on local online catalogues can also be helpful. The Hospital Records Database provides details of the location of hospitals, many of which began as charitable or voluntary foundations. For example, the registers of admission for the Foundling Hospital (with the tokens deposited by the babies' mothers) are now at the London Metropolitan Archives, along with other records of the hospital.

By the nineteenth century, as the population increased, so had the problem of destitute children. A number of charities and philanthropists stepped in. One of the best known was Thomas Barnardo, originally an evangelical missionary to the East End. He set up children's homes in the East End with the phrase 'No destitute child

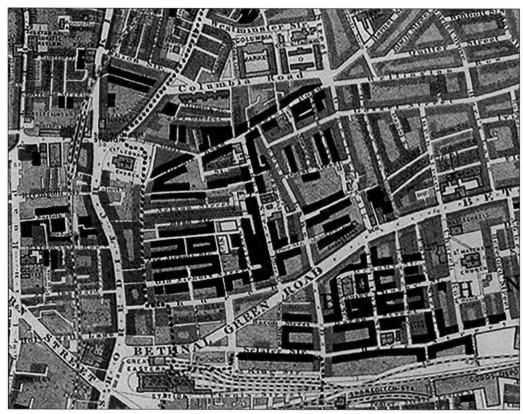

Part of Charles Booth's poverty map, published in 1889 in *Life and Labour of the People in London*. It shows the Old Nichol, a slum in the East End of London. Originally published on colour, different shading indicates levels of poverty, ranging from 'middle class, well-to-do' through 'poor, 18s to 21s a week for a moderate family' and 'very poor, casual, chronic want', to the 'lowest class ... occasional labourers, street sellers, loafers, criminals and semi-criminals' (darker shading). *(Wikimedia Commons)*

refused admission' above the door and provided many other services for poor children. By the time of his death in 1905 the charity ran ninety-six homes across Britain caring for over 8,500 children. Charities like this, which are still in existence, tend to keep their own archives, which (sometimes for a fee) you can request to look at. Barnardo's, for instance, maintains a large archive which has detailed records about all the children it helped from the 1870s. If you had a relative you believe was in the care of Barnardo's during their child-hood, they may have records and images of that ancestor.

Another useful digital archive is Hidden Lives Revealed, which is an archive of children cared for by the Waifs and Strays Society. It includes examples of 150 case files, although the names of the children have been anonymised (which is obviously an issue for researchers tracing specific individuals), despite some cases being over 100 years old (see the discussion of ethics at the end of this chapter). Therefore, although this archive holds a range of archive material, its stance on anonymity means that not all of its holdings are accessible to the public. Nevertheless, the site has information on children's homes up to the 1980s, focusing particularly on the period 1881–1918. The Society cared for children across England and Wales in both rural and urban settings. To illustrate its size, around 22,500 children were looked after by the Waifs and Strays' Society between 1882 and 1918. The Waifs and Strays' Society became the Church of England Children's Society in 1946 and is now known as The Children's Society. Photographs can be viewed that demonstrate the poverty of the time, and also show how children's lives changed when they entered the Society's care. Also featured on the site are the texts of various Society publications and the organisation's Annual Reports. While not all individual lives can be viewed, the site does offer information about the Victorian and Edwardian social order, including poverty; working, social and familial lives; child welfare laws; how the Society cared for disabled children and integrated them into society; and how social support charities worked with local communities. The case studies that are available to view include an application form which provides information including details about the child and their family, where and when they were born, and the health, education, ages, occupations and wages of family members. A description of the child's circumstances and the reason for seeking a place with the Society is also given. The files also contain other material, such as letters from the child's family and even from the children themselves, newspaper clippings, letters from prisons and lunatic asylums, photographs, school reports and apprenticeship indenture documents. As with most historical documents, some case files contain more information than others – some cover the brief period of the child's life up to entering the Society, while others range over sixty years, enabling researchers to explore life outcomes. Such a long period is available for some individuals because whenever information on a former resident reached the Society, they added it to the file. There are, of course, many other children's institutions and archival sites available that are not mentioned here.

Recreating Children's Lives

Using a combination of the criminal and non-criminal records described earlier it is usually possible to piece together the fragmented lives of juvenile offenders. This method of concentrating on an individual's life-course is not without its criticism. Looking across the whole of one person's life is not just a matter of finding enough information; there is also the problem of providing the proper amount of context. Only if we know what was going on in wider society (and in the criminal justice system) in that period can we really understand how a person's life was affected by those changing conditions. In order to do this, primary sources including official statistical returns, parliamentary reports and correspondence of those in authority should also be used for detailed research projects (such as a postgraduate qualification). Fortunately, there are plenty of books which summarise the main changes that took place in the criminal justice system in the nineteenth and twentieth centuries (see Further Reading). This allows broader aspects of society, such as the economy, offending and punishment patterns, education, health, mortality and population changes, to be explored. Only then is it possible to approach an understanding of the lives uncovered.

We are unfortunately not awash with diaries and first-person accounts of the nineteenth- and early twentieth-century working classes. That is not to say all working classes were illiterate prior to the Education Act of 1870, but any ability in reading and writing did not generally result in the production of an account of their lives. Some do exist, however, such as Brendan Behan's autobiography *Borstal Boy*, which recounts first-hand experiences of incarceration. Where available, such accounts can be used to add to the understanding of individual experiences of different punishments. However, it is often the case, as with Brendan Behan (who was a well-educated political prisoner), that those who leave autobiographies are not representative of those imprisoned with them. Consequently, the lives of the working classes are difficult to uncover, and those of their children even more so.

Through uncovering the lives of young convicts it is possible to reveal the events of criminality and punishment, which allows an assessment of whether or not criminality was embedded in a person's whole-life course, or (as crime historians argue) was merely a temporary phase. Were the crimes they committed in youth only a part (and often a small part) of their whole lives? Through using the criminal records outlined above, combined with newspapers and civil records, it is possible to reconstruct these juvenile convicts' lives in order to answer these important questions.

Telling the Story

While the life-narratives of juvenile offenders are of interest, the crimes which initiated many juvenile criminal careers are far from extra-ordinary and therefore their biographical narratives should not be romanticised. This is particularly a challenge given the youth and the petty nature of many of their crimes. However, this can be avoided by remaining true to the facts and avoiding any interpretation of the offenders' narratives with the attitude of giving them 'the benefit of the doubt'. By contextualising the juveniles' lives and stressing, for example, that while today's society would consider their crimes re-markably petty, for example pickpocketing a handkerchief, contem-poraries saw property crime as a serious offence and pickpocketing specifically as the 'gateway' to more serious offences (such as burg-lary and robbery). It must be remembered that these juvenile offen-ders had 'agency'. They made decisions, even if they were poor ones, or were desperate choices from a poor range of available options. While some juveniles stole food to survive and others were arrested for vagrancy (essentially being poor and homeless), still others chose to steal or commit crimes for a variety of reasons including peer pres-sure, excitement and boredom.

What Can We Learn?

In producing case studies (Chapter Five), we can gain some under-standing of the reasons why some children committed crimes, and we get an idea of how hard some children found the transition into adult-hood. We also have details of how the criminal justice system treated children who broke the law in this period. How can we use this infor-mation? To what purpose can it be put? Although it would be nice to think that the Prime Minister will read this book and come up with a solution to the problem of juvenile delinquency, it's unlikely that this will happen. We think that this book might serve two purposes, how-ever. First, it should (if we have done our job) provide some informa-tion on the subject which is new, interesting and informative; it may even challenge existing views on delinquency. Second, we hope that it will encourage readers to find out more information about children (the transported, the imprisoned, and those confined in industrial schools and reformatories) for their own research purposes. A huge number of people have someone in their family tree who was caught up in the juvenile justice system. We hope that this book will not only provide more information about their experiences in general, but also equip readers with the tools to discover more details about specific juvenile offenders. Readers should beware, however, for as the next section shows it is easy to wander straight into an ethical minefield.

Ethics

As researchers and readers, we are always reading someone else's stories. Sometimes they involve our own family, and sometimes they are about someone else's family. We might get upset if we read something that seems to be critical of our ancestors, or we discover a skeleton in the closet that we don't want to become public knowledge, or if someone gets a 'fact' wrong about a great-grandfather or someone even further back in the family line. We may get just as annoyed about wrong information being told about someone we are not related to, or had never heard of until we read their story. Our trade is data, and, in this book perhaps more than many others, that data comes from private official records that were never intended to be revealed. They carry secrets that were never meant to be told to living descendants (or to anybody else outside the criminal justice system). Finding out that you are related to one of the boys and girls mentioned in this book might turn out to be what researchers label 'uncalled-for knowledge'. It can be a shock to discover that one's ancestors committed unsavoury crimes. Even if you are not personally related to someone in this book, it can still be unsettling.

So, we have had to think about a number of things in writing this book. Anyone researching the history of crime and punishment, or the history of childhood, will have come across similar issues.

The first issue is whether to anonymise the people in this book. We have not given a pseudonym to each child, although we have anonymised the names of some victims. Although this is the easiest way to avoid any ethical problems – giving someone a false name almost renders the story a piece of fiction – it also robs us as researchers of two things: the right to be told the truth, and the ability to do our own further research on the case when more documents come to light. It also prevents the child having their story told. We have not anonymised Brendan Behan because he wants his story told – he wrote an autobiography, and reached a wide audience with his life story (told in his own words, and on his own terms), but not everyone had the opportunity to do that. We did make a small number of exceptions to our 'anonymity rule'. For example, we hid the names of some cases because they died comparatively recently. Why did we do this?

This is because it seemed to us that their story was so recent that their children (in one case their son would be in his eighties) or more realistically their grand-children (who may or may not know the story of their relative's past crimes and indiscretions) could read about their crimes. We decided that people who had battled to escape their difficult and troubled pasts deserved to be left in peace. As was said in *Young Criminal Lives* in 2017:

> these people 'were more than their official record; they were brothers, sons, fathers and grandfathers. They were workers, soldiers, farmers, factory workers and shop-workers. They played as children, they were sometimes ill, they grew old and received pensions, and some died for their country.' Gerald Bardsley died at Ypres in the First World War. Should he not be remembered for his wartime efforts as much as for his singular criminal conviction? Should his real name be removed from our book? That is what we have done; George Bardsley's name is a pseudonym, a fiction, even if his deeds were real.

You may disagree with our decision, and we recognise that everyone is entitled to make up their own mind about this issue.

Let us throw up one more thing to think about, though. You may be reading this book because you have an interest in youth crime, in the history of children in this period, or because you have found a person in your family tree who committed a crime as a youth, and it has thrown up new questions. How do I find out more about that person? How do I find out more about their experiences in prison or an Australian penal colony? You may be an experienced researcher, an avid reader of contemporary literature and archival documents, or you may just have a passing interest. We are all of us now privileged in that we can find a huge amount of information on young criminals online. The digital revolution very easily gives us access to court cases, prison records and sometimes to juvenile offenders' records. Although we have put together a lot of digital data from various sources, and also supplemented that with archival documents, it would be easy for readers to construct their own life-histories (with some care and a lot of time). The case for anonymising names in books and articles may soon be taken out of our hands with the click of a mouse, and other people might decide to take a different course of action from us and publish names and places in any case.

CHAPTER FIVE

LIFE STORIES

1. John Hudson (b.1774) and William Gadsby (b.1822)

Emerging from the dark and grim conditions of Newgate Prison, where he had been kept for three months on remand until his trial was possible, John Hudson was brought to the Old Bailey on 10 December 1783. He is thought to have been 9 years old when he was charged with breaking and entering a house in East Smithfield, London, at night. Night-time burglaries were always treated more seriously, and could attract the death sentence. John was accused of stealing from William Holdsworth's house one linen shirt valued at ten shillings, five silk stockings valued at five shillings, a pistol also valued at five shillings, and some aprons.

There were three main pieces of evidence ranged against him. First, at the scene of the burglary there were small sooty footprints and toe-marks on the window shutter. When John was apprehended he was trying to wash himself clean of soot. He was employed as a chimney sweep, and may have been washing away the soot from his work. However, as a chimney sweep, he would also have been adept at squeezing himself into small spaces – useful in committing burglaries. Second, the cellar where John was sleeping contained many of the missing items, including the pistol, which was in the very sink where John was washing himself. This was fairly conclusive, but most damning of all, the pawnbroker identified John as the boy who had brought one of the stolen items into the pawnshop.

At his trial he had no one to defend him and he spoke only a total of thirteen words:

'How old are you?'
'Going on nine.'
'What business was you bred up in?'
'None, sometimes a chimney sweeper.'
'Have you any father or mother?'
'Dead.'
'How long ago?'
'I do not know.'

This small exchange of questions and answers seems to have been sufficient to convince the court that John was 'adult' enough to understand why he was there, and that he was responsible for his actions. As Chapter Two noted, children had to be assessed to see if they were *doli capax* or *incapax* before standing trial. The Old Bailey considered John to be *doli capax* (aware that he had committed a crime rather than just being naughty). Nonetheless, the judge seems to have had some sympathy for the 9-year-old boy:

> The boy's confession may be admitted, in evidence, but we must take it with every allowance, and at the utmost it only proves he was in the house; now he might have got in after daybreak, as the prosecutor was not informed of it till eight the next morning. The only thing that fixes this boy with the robbery is the pistol found in the sink; that might not have been put there by the boy: his confession with respect to how he came there, I do not think should be allowed, because it was made under fear; I think it would be too hard to find a boy of his tender age guilty of the burglary; one would wish to snatch such a boy, if one possibly could, from destruction, for he will only return to the same kind of life which he has led before, and will be an instrument in the hands of very bad people, who make use of boys of that sort to rob houses ... He is sentenced to seven years' transportation.

The *Mercury* waited for him in the dock ready to sail to America. From the seventeenth century the American colonies had received about 50,000 convicts (the exact figure is unknown) in order to provide free labour. The War of Independence largely, but not completely, ended the convict trade. The 'dumping' of convicts had been a source of complaint by American revolutionaries, although when the government-sponsored system ended, private companies took up the trade and it continued until 1785. John boarded the *Mercury* on 30 March 1784 but the ship never sailed. There was a mutiny on board and John was disembarked and sent to the *Dunkirk* hulk in Plymouth in June.

The hulks were a short-term solution to an emerging crisis. With the American colonies now refusing to take convicts, ships began to be moored in the Thames and elsewhere to act as holding bays until a new place for forced convict emigration could be found. The hulks were mast-less warships which were old, unsanitary and riven with disease. The sick were given little medical attention and were not separated from the healthy, so diseases like typhoid (known as gaol fever) spread very quickly and were hard to eradicate. The officers who guarded the prisoners on the hulks were often removed at night for their own safety, the near-naked adult and child prisoners being locked into pens until morning. Sexual predation may have been high, and the superintendent of the *Dunkirk* complained to the authorities on 25 August 1784 that the female prisoners were often sexually assaulted by the Marines who were supposed to be guarding them.

Respite, of a kind, was near at hand for the prisoners on the *Dunkirk*. With America no longer an option, the Australian colonies offered a possible solution. Home Secretary Lord Sydney looked to create a convict colony at Botany Bay, on the eastern coast of New South Wales, under the command of Captain Arthur Phillip. John changed ships and was placed on the *Friendship*, moored at Portsmouth, on 5 March 1787, with eighty male and two female prisoners.

By the time the First Fleet sailed to New South Wales, John had been on the *Defence* for three years. Second Lieutenant Ralph Clark of the Royal Marines mis-recorded John's name on the ship's roster (as Thomas not John) and there is very little further information available about John. He can be found on board the *Sirius* bound for Norfolk Island (a penal colony) on 4 March 1790 and received fifty lashes for breaching his convict curfew (being out of his hut after nine o'clock) on 15 February 1791. Was he the same John Hudson who is recorded as being at Port Jackson on 24 October 1795? We will never know.

What we *do* know is that John's life took many twists and turns, most of which were out of his hands. He may have taken the decision to offend when he was aged 9, but it is impossible to tell whether he was coerced, or whether he could really understand the implications and possible consequences of his actions. The court thought so, and desired to send him away from British shores. His intended voyage to America never materialised, and he was diverted many times before reaching his new home in New South Wales. The direction his life took was decided by others, and rested on small decisions with big impacts. Young boys like John who ended up in the criminal justice system had little power, and were subject to the will of others.

* * *

If we move forward exactly fifty years to examine the life of William Gadsby, another young boy who stood in the Old Bailey dock aged 11, we see that not much had changed in that regard.

Holborn-born William Gadsby was tried in 1833 at London's Central Criminal Court (https://www.digitalpanopticon.org/life?id=obpt18331017-49-defend554). He was accused of stealing nearly five shillings in cash from his father, also named William. This was the kind of theft that would be moved to the magistrates' courts by the 1855 Criminal Justice Act (see Chapter Two). However, as it was, William was tried alongside murderers and rapists at the Old Bailey.

William's father was a hackney-coachman (a London taxi-driver) who lived with his wife Elizabeth and 11-year-old William. William Senior testified in court that 'on the 24th of September I called him [his son] up, at seven o'clock in the morning, to light the fire and get breakfast'. The father had some money in his coat pocket that he had earned the night before. When he looked for the money in the morning, it had gone. So had his son. In fact, he did not manage to track down his son for another fortnight. He told the court that his son had stolen money from him six or seven times before, and that he now wanted his son to be prosecuted. This seems like the actions of a father who was at the end of his tether – he declared that he had tried to 'reclaim' his son many times in the past, but to no avail.

The court found William guilty and the judge sentenced him to seven years' transportation. Like John Hudson, he was first sent to a hulk to await a ship to take him to Van Diemen's Land. Perhaps bearing out what his father had said in court, his behaviour on the hulk was described as 'indifferent'. He was transported on the *Norfolk* out of Sheerness on 12 May 1835.

The convict records of Van Diemen's Land tell us that he earned his ticket of leave (a conditional pardon allowing him certain freedoms) on 14 May 1840, and he was granted a full certificate of freedom just a few months later, on 17 October 1840. He was aged 19 at this point. Most convicts earned their ticket of leave much earlier in their sentence. Why had William's been delayed? A clue is found in the *Tasmanian Weekly Despatch* which reported that William Gadsby's ticket of leave had been suspended (taken away for a period) on 26 June 1840, and that he had been sentenced to two months' hard labour for misconduct whilst at work. Perhaps William continued to be 'indifferent' towards his supervisors and his new employer during his time in the penal colony.

Like John Hudson, William then disappears from history. We do not know whether he reformed, or continued to get into trouble; indeed, we know very little about his life as an adult. There is a report of a William Gadsby dying in the Victorian goldmines, back on the Australian mainland, a few years later. The *Ballarat Star* reported that William Gadsby had died in hospital from injuries received through being run over by a waggon. Was this 'our' William? Again, this will never be known. John Hudson and William Gadsby will both remain in the records as children sent overseas at the whim of the courts, but who then disappeared from the pages of history.

2. Letitia Padwick (b.1815)

Letitia was born in Kingston, London, in 1815. By the 1830s she had secured a job working as a domestic servant for a grocer in the neighbourhood. Letitia, like thousands of other girls and young women, endured long working hours and poor wages, but enjoyed a fair amount of freedom on a daily basis. Her work duties allowed her to roam the house, and the poor pay made theft a constant temptation. Many domestic servants who succumbed to those temptations were punished informally; often they were dismissed from service and denied a reference, which would have made getting another job very difficult. When Letitia was accused of theft, her employer decided to prosecute her. Aged 17, she appeared in the dock at the Old Bailey in April 1832. London's Central Criminal Court (the Old Bailey) would have been an impressive and frightening place for Letitia, who had probably never been in so grand a building.

George Hodgkinson gave his evidence first. He stated that he was a grocer who had employed Letitia as a house-servant. When he started to notice that some of his property was going missing, he searched her belongings and found some of his own. He then went to Letitia's mother's house and found some missing parcels of tea. The Metropolitan Police had been formed in 1829 and Hodgkinson took the opportunity to contact the local 'bobby'. The case against Letitia, which looked strong at the beginning, started to fall apart when the tea was found to have no identifying marks on it. How could Mr Hodgkinson prove it was his tea? He couldn't, and the case against Letitia was dismissed. She wasn't yet off the hook, however.

On the same day and in the same court she faced a second charge of stealing from her master. She was accused of taking two shirts valued at eleven shillings (about a week's wages for Letitia), six chocolate cakes valued at four shillings, some cocoa, almonds, starch and other grocery items which totalled up to about three or four pounds in value. There was also some tea, which again was not identified as belonging to Mr Hodgkinson, but by this point it was becoming harder for Letitia to maintain that all of the items were actually hers. And then the shirts were produced, all with 'Hodgkinson' written on the inside label. The game was up. Letitia admitted that she had stolen the property and threw herself on the mercy of the court. The Judge imposed a sentence of fourteen years' transportation.

Letitia and five of her friends and family petitioned for clemency on her behalf. Such petitions, which are now kept at the National Archives in London (HO 17/3/104), were usually sent directly to the Home Office, which acted on behalf of the crown. The Home Office forwarded the petition and any supporting documents to the trial judge or the Recorder of London (when cases had been decided in the Old Bailey, as Letitia's was) asking for a report and their own personal recommendation. The Home Office tended to go along with the judge's recommendation in most cases. The petition for the revocation or at least the reduction of Letitia's sentence stressed that she was very young, and had not conspired with anyone else in her crimes. They added that her friends and family were respectable people and had no knowledge of her activities. Her aged father would be devastated by his daughter being sent away for so long. Lastly, her prosecutor had offered to take her back into service if she was not transported. The Home Office considered the petition but eventually Letitia sailed on the convict transport vessel *Frances Charlotte* on 30 August 1832 to start her fourteen-year penal servitude sentence in Van Diemen's Land. When she arrived in what would later become Tasmania (the island changed its name in 1856 to try to escape its reputation as a penal colony), she would have served time in the female factory in Hobart.

The Cascades Female Factory in Hobart was opened in 1828 to hold convict women (usually women who had committed further offences after arriving in the colony). The factory segregated women from the (mainly alcohol-related) entertainments available in Hobart, and also from the male convicts. Located in a damp, low-lying part of town, the accommodation was cramped, overcrowded and dirty, and contagious diseases were easily spread through the factory's dormitories. The mortality rate was high among the women held there. By the time the Cascades Female Factory closed in 1856, Letitia was long gone. When she left the factory, she would have been sent on assignment to an employer. This meant a return to domestic service for Letitia, and another stint of hard work. Her life was not without enjoyment or support, however.

The records of the Tasmanian Archives and Heritage Office reveal that Letitia made a second petition in 1834, seeking permission to marry her lover David George. The court and convict records also tell

The Female Factory from Proctor's Quarry (1844); detail showing the Cascades Female Factory in Hobart, Van Diemen's Land (now Tasmania), hand-coloured lithograph by John Skinner Prout (1805–1876). (*Wikimedia Commons*)

us a little bit about David's life too. He was eight years younger than Letitia. Born in 1807, he was indicted at the Old Bailey on 27 October 1825. His victim, Matthew Wilson, stated that he felt 'a pull at my coat-pocket, and turned round; I saw the prisoner and another person – each of them had hold of my silk handkerchief; I collared them both, but being very weak, I let the other go, and kept the prisoner.' David countered that he was not near the victim when the handkerchief was taken, and then changed his story. 'Why did you let the other man go?' he asked, and then said that the victim had threatened to pummel him to the ground as he was small. Unimpressed with the evidence, the judge announced the sentence: he was to be transported for life. His appeal for clemency was also turned down, and he sailed on the *Earl St Vincent*, arriving in 1826.

With a five-year head start over Letitia, and a ticket of leave from 1835, David would have been more familiar with convict conditions and the skills needed to survive in the penal colony. He may have been a comforting and very useful person to have in Letitia's life. It certainly would have been a hard life for an unmarried young woman. Letitia and David, aged 17 and 19 respectively, must have clung together to try to make the best of their situations. Neither of them reoffended in their new land as far as we are aware. There are no Australian newspaper reports of any trials, and no criminal records that we can find.

Letitia experienced several huge upheavals in her life, starting from her sentence of transportation when she was just a teenager. When the judge said 'fourteen years', it may have sounded like a life sentence to Letitia, and it was certainly the start of a long period of punishment, disgrace, discomfort and hard work, but she also managed to find a new relationship and forge a new life as an honest woman in Tasmania. Just as she must have thought her life had stabilised as a married woman, David and Letitia's life together was cut short when David died in 1855, aged just 48. Letitia was back on her own again, but as a grown woman this time, rather than a teenage girl. Although we know very little about the rest of her life in the colony, Letitia may well have married again (women who could not rely on a male wage-earner to support them could end up destitute and living out their days in poverty) and she may, at last, have found some peace and stability in her life.

3. William Asgill (1824–1875)

Born in Bayswater, London, in 1824, William Asgill experienced an early taste of confinement in Newgate Prison (https://www.digital panopticon.org/life?id=obpdef1-1501-18360613). By this time, Newgate had been rebuilt after it had been severely damaged in the 1780 Gordon Riots. The new design was laid out around a central courtyard, with an area designated for poor prisoners and another area for those able to afford more comfortable accommodation. Intended to house debtors and convicted prisoners, Newgate also held prisoners like William who were awaiting trial at the Old Bailey.

William, an 11-year-old boy with light brown hair, hazel eyes and a fresh complexion, was charged with the theft of tools on 13 June 1836. The victim, Mr Humphreys, was a wheelwright who suspected the boy, and when he missed his saws and other tools he contacted a local beadle. The beadle handed William over to a constable to be arrested and charged.

This was a good example of collaboration between the outgoing and incoming models of policing. The beadles were part of the locally organised and locally funded parish watchmen who guarded individual neighbourhoods in London and other cities. The proponents of the Metropolitan Police portrayed the watchmen as old, inefficient and corrupt. The Metropolitan Police, introduced in 1829, comprised men who were supposed to be younger, fitter and more suited to policing the largest city in the world.

However, the beadles and watchmen did have their defenders. Dickens was a supporter, of sorts:

> The parish beadle is one of the most, perhaps THE most, important member of the local administration. He is not so well off as the churchwardens, certainly, nor is he so learned as the vestry-clerk, nor does he order things quite so much his own way as either of them. But his power is very great, notwithstanding; and the dignity of his office is never impaired by the absence of efforts on his part to maintain it.
>
> (Charles Dickens, *Sketches by Boz*, 1839)

Modern historians have also suggested that the beadles were not so inefficient, and the new bobbies not so efficient, as is often assumed. They suggest that the two systems muddled along together, with the Londoners they all served making use of whoever came to hand when they needed some law and order, until the 1840s.

After William had been arrested, a police sergeant was surprised to hear a thumping on the station-house door. William had an offer for him. 'Will you be so kind as to send for the gentleman who charged me, and I will tell him where the saws are?' William stated that they were hidden up the chimney in one of the half-built houses near the station-house. Since the police could not find them, William kindly escorted them back to the house and showed them exactly where the saws were hidden. William's defence in court – that another young lad had simply showed him where the stolen goods had been squirrelled away – was not very convincing. He was found guilty and sentenced to seven years' transportation.

Like many others, he was first taken to a hulk to wait for a transport ship to take him to Van Diemen's Land. The report on him said that he had to be flogged for indiscipline on the hulk, and his behaviour was described as 'indifferent'. That was also the term used by the surgeon-superintendent on his transport ship, the *Frances Charlotte*. At sea, usually for between three and six months, the surgeon-superintendents were supposed to regulate the health of the convicts and the general living conditions on the ship. Their influence and powers grew as the convict system developed. In the nineteenth century surgeons were selected from the Royal Navy and were given ultimate authority over the convicts during the voyage. They were allowed to prevent sickly prisoners from boarding, which helped to prevent contagious diseases from spreading as quickly as they did on the hulks, and they generally increased the survival rate of convicts reaching Australia.

Alexander Nesbitt, the surgeon-superintendent on the *Frances Charlotte*, was entered in the Navy List of Medical Officers in 1814. He appears to have been an interesting man. A report in *The Times* in 1829 described an incident between Nesbitt and a fellow-passenger, Mr Dawson, who was travelling back to England on board a convict transport which had deposited its human cargo. Mr Nesbitt was the surgeon-superintendent on the outboard trip and was also returning home. One evening, at tea, the conversation between these two passengers turned to the characteristics of tropical winds. Indeed, their argument grew as heated as the winds they discussed, and Nesbitt punched Mr Dawson on the nose without warning. He then expressed his regret for the blow he had given him, and invited the plaintiff to shake hands and forget the incident. Mr Dawson declined the offer and instead took Nesbitt to court for assault. Being a gentleman rather than one of the convicts he was used to treating, Nesbitt paid Dawson £100 by way of apology and damages. Later he survived a shipwreck when the *Royal Charlotte* was wrecked in 1825, and served on a number of convict vessels before becoming a land-based surgeon at Greenwich Hospital in London.

William reached Van Diemen's Land in January 1837, and his convict record states that he was convicted of an offence in the colony. This meant he was sent to Port Arthur, which was designed to hold and punish those who reoffended after transportation. William received his certificate of freedom on 13 June 1843. That is where his convict record ends, and we can gain little more from his official record. However, as is sometimes the case, descendants and family historians have added information as it becomes available (https: //convictrecords.com.au/convicts/asgill/william/16247). A contributor has added that William was convicted of larceny (theft) on 24 April 1865 for which he received a custodial sentence with hard labour. He was living at that time at Oatlands, a town halfway between Hobart and Launceston. Oatlands was mainly constructed by convicts while under sentence. The now-picturesque Tasmanian town actually has the largest number of colonial buildings of any town in Australia. Aged 46, William succumbed to 'Serious apoplexy' at the general hospital in Hobart and died on 28 December 1875. He was buried at the Cornelian Bay Cemetery, in the part of the burial ground reserved for paupers.

4. Ellen Miles alias Smith/Jackson (b.1827)

Born in 1827, Ellen was 12 years of age when she was convicted at the Old Bailey and sentenced to transportation for seven years for uttering counterfeit coin. (Uttering was the process of putting counterfeit coin into circulation.) This was not her first offence: Ellen had been brought before the courts for uttering when she was just 10 years old but her judgment was respited after she pleaded guilty. The *Taunton Courier and Western Advertiser* referred to Ellen as 'A Young Hopeful'. The article stated that at the guildhall Ellen Miles was charged with passing a counterfeit half-crown to a shop-keeper in Russell Street. The newspaper pointed out that Ellen was one of three sisters whose mother had died, 'all notorious utterers'. The article asserted that Ellen had been in custody thirty times and was only discharged the previous week. The newspaper further added that she had been convicted at the Old Bailey previously and if convicted again she would be transported. Claiming he was unable to control her, Ellen's father suggested that it would be an act of mercy to transport her. Instead, Alderman Lainson discharged Ellen with a warning. While records of thirty custodial sentences could not be located, Ellen had certainly been confined previously for fourteen days and on this occasion it was eventually decided, in May 1839, that she would be kept in prison for six months' imprisonment at the House of Correction in Clerkenwell and set to hard labour. It was recommended by the court that she be made known to the Children's Friends Society, which was focused on diverting juveniles out of the penal system (see Chapter Three). Despite this recommendation, it was added that Ellen's sentence was for 'too short a time'. However, the newspapers were correct. Ellen was transported, after a further offence later that same year, on board the female convict ship *Gilbert Henderson* in December 1839. Ellen was 13 years old by the time she arrived in Hobart. Even at the age of 12 Ellen had been shrewd enough to attempt, albeit unsuccessfully, to use an alias, giving both 'Smith' and 'Jackson' as her surname, presumably in an attempt to prevent her previous court appearances being connected to her, and in doing so escape a harsher punishment.

Ellen arrived in Hobart in April 1840. After just two months in the colony she committed her first offence, 'insolence and disobedience of orders', for which she received six days' solitary confinement. Consequently she was removed from her assignment to the cells. The offences which followed included disobedience of orders, neglect of duty, insolence, repeatedly being absent and absconding, disorderly conduct, being found in company with a man by the name of Richard Nichols, destroying property and creating disturbance in the gaol, and, perhaps more seriously, larceny (although only taking things of small value). In total Ellen committed eighteen separate offences. Most of these were regulatory offences, meaning they would not have been classed as offences if Ellen were not a convict. However, this was more offending than usual for a female convict and Ellen certainly did steal; furthermore, absconding was considered a serious offence. These offences led to punishments such as solitary confinement, but she was also put to hard labour in the criminal class at the female house of correction (known as female factories; see Chapter Three). When Ellen absconded, her original sentence of transportation was extended by six months, and for two months of this extension Ellen was to be detained in the house of correction on probation. Initially after each offence Ellen was reassigned to a free settler relatively quickly. However, after her extension of sentence in September 1842 she seems to have spent the majority of her time confined. Still, by November 1844 Ellen was at the hiring depot ready for reassignment. Ellen's offending at this point had slowed down when she was sent out of assignment and back into Cascades, the female factory in Hobart, for six months. Despite recurrent offences, Ellen was repeatedly reassigned following her punishment. As well as Cascades, Ellen also spent time at the Launceston Female Factory.

Ellen was free by servitude by April 1847, after her full seven years' sentence was complete. Described as a 'slightly poke-pitted' 'nurse girl', four and a half feet tall when she arrived in Van Diemen's Land, Ellen grew up there and applied for permission to marry in August 1847 just four months after gaining freedom. In March 1848 Ellen was married at Melville Chapel to Thomas Watkins. Thomas had arrived in Van Diemen's Land on the *Runnymede* but was a ticket-of-leave holder when the pair married. He was working as a costermonger (selling fruit and vegetables from a handcart) at the time of their first child's birth. Ellen was 21 years of age when she married, and Thomas was only slightly her senior at 23. Ellen could neither read nor write before her arrival in Van Diemen's Land but by the time she was married she was able to sign the marriage register. They had at least one child, whom they named after the father, born in August 1847.

Ellen's repeated offences led to her spending the bulk of her sentence in confinement. As such, Ellen only married when she reached freedom. Many female convicts, if they were single, married while still under sentence, a process which often allowed them to be assigned to their husbands, removing them to some degree from the penal system. This was a sensible plan if the husband was a good man. While she had to wait until she gained her freedom, Ellen did marry and produced a family almost immediately. However, her offending career was not over. There is evidence, as reported in the *Argus* newspaper in 1836, that she and her husband were involved in a highway robbery in Victoria. Later, it was reported in the *Kilmore Free Press* that she was brought before the Kilmore Police Court in 1896 for stealing a coat, a charge to which she pleaded guilty and was sentenced to one month in Melbourne Gaol. Taken in conjunction with possible vagrancy charges in her old age, it would seem Ellen's colonial life was not settled. However, many female juveniles arriving as convicts forged pathways which led them away from their criminal pasts and enabled them to live normal, working-class lives free from crime.

5. James McAllister (1827–1855)

The life and crimes of James McAllister began relatively unremarkably until he completed his transportation sentence and was executed in Australia. Born in 1827, James was brought to trial in 1842 for stealing sixty pence, aged 14. He was sentenced to seven years' transportation while his accomplice, aged 16, was sentenced to two months' imprisonment. There were no former convictions mentioned at his trial, but his conduct record states that he stole loaves, for which he received three weeks' confinement, and a waistcoat for which he spent another fourteen days in the house of correction. Also of note is that he was admitted to the Workhouse twice in the couple of years prior to his Old Bailey appearance and was described as having 'no home'. His conduct record confirms what this phrase suggests. While James did have two brothers and two aunts in London, he had no parents at this time. He did have employment as a mariner and/or labourer at some point but clearly he had a difficult start. As such he could neither read nor write and he was also hesitant in his speech.

Even at the time of his death he was described as being able to read and write only very imperfectly.

His behaviour was described as 'orderly' on board the *Euryalus* and 'good' by the ship's surgeon-superintendent during the voyage. James only had to wait five months until he sailed on board the *Asiatic*. Arriving in Hobart in 1843, he was put on probation for two years at Point Puer. While some juvenile convicts filled their conduct records with offences while under sentence, James committed only one offence, which was 'Misconduct in being concealed in the enclosed yard of Mr. Johnson for some unlawful purpose' in 1849, while a ticket-of-leave holder. This was six years after his arrival; prior to this he had committed no offences and had only earned his ticket of leave that year. He was given three months' hard labour and ordered not to reside in Hobart Town. He finally received his certificate of freedom in 1850. It seemed to be a great start for James in the colony but just five years later he found himself in Melbourne Gaol awaiting execution for the murder of Jane Jones.

During this period James had made his way to Melbourne working as a labourer and carpenter. The newspapers stated that he had adopted the 'most disreputable means of getting a living since he has been in this colony'. He was at that time running a lodging house, although the newspapers suggested that this was a brothel (later confirmed by the dying words of Jane Jones). He was not married and had no known children. He had, however, cohabited for two years with Jane Jones prior to shooting her. Jane was shot at the Exchange Hotel in March 1855 and later died in hospital of her injuries. She made a statement before she died, explaining that the prisoner was not the father of her child and that he had shot her because she refused to live with him. In fact, a month prior to the evening of the shooting, Jane had left James to live with another man named Thomas Chisholm, an article clerk. Jane told Chisholm that James had ill-used and threatened her. Jane and Thomas Chisholm had to move lodgings because they saw James watching Jane. On one occasion he stopped her in the street and took her child from her and struck her. Consequently, he was summoned before the City Police court and was ordered to give the child back to the mother.

On the night of the shooting, Thomas Chisholm was out. On returning, he saw James, who levelled a pistol at him and fired. Fortunately for Thomas, the bullet merely grazed his temple, sending him falling backwards. As Thomas began to get up, he heard another pistol shot. James had shot Jane. James initially tried to run, but a waiter stopped him and he then surrendered himself, declaring 'I am the murderer.' Jane had been shot in the shoulder, but a second bullet, lodged in her spinal cord, causing paralysis and later death. Jane was only 22 years old and described as 'of plain appearance', while James was described as 'respectable looking'. At trial, the defence admitted the act but argued that the crime was not murder but manslaughter because James could not be held responsible for his actions because he was provoked. The provocation, they claimed, was that he had been made furious because Jane was, to all intents and purposes, his wife and she had eloped with another man. Seeing the man who had taken her, he was not able to control his actions. The judge disagreed, pointing out that he could see no provocation for manslaughter and commenting that there was nothing to suggest they were as good as married. The jury returned a verdict of wilful murder against James McAllister and he was executed at Melbourne Gaol.

Approximately 500 people were present outside the gaol to witness the execution. James was one of the 113 people executed in Melbourne Gaol (one of the others was the notorious bushranger Ned Kelly). However, no one but the officials was allowed to be present within the walls at the time of the execution. James apparently approached his death with resignation, which was consistent with his general behaviour since being sentenced. He was said to have conducted himself with humility and apparent penitence, and expressed no hope of pardon in this world. A cast of his head was reported to have been taken by an artist, Mr Pardoe, after death.

6. John Lee (b.1829)

John Lee first appears in the records after being convicted of stealing apples. This offence resulted in fourteen days' confinement and was followed by another conviction for stealing spoons, which resulted in two months' confinement. He appears to have spent one week in Westminster Gaol but it is unclear for what offence. By the age of 12 John was brought before the Old Bailey in March 1841, charged with stealing four spoons from Charles Danieli's shop in Oxford Street, with another juvenile, 16-year-old George Hambley. Joseph Mount, a police constable, stated:

> ... I saw the two prisoners together – they went to the shop of Mr Danieli, in Oxford Street, and lifted up a glass case outside

the shop; Lee took out three spoons and Hambley took one – they ran away, I and my brother officer pursued and took them – they threw down the spoons, which we took up.

While George declared: 'There were two others who took the spoons, and they [mis]took us for them', John remained silent. They were both found guilty. John was sentenced to seven years' transportation, and the judge specified he would be sent to a 'convict ship', rather than to Parkhurst Prison (a prison for juveniles on the Isle of Wight). George Hambley was given the same sentence.

John's mother, Ellen Lee, had a petition written on her behalf which stressed that she was broken-hearted and wanted her son to stay in the country. John had two sisters named Kitty and Ellen, with whom he lived in Castle Lane, London. Before his conviction he was employed as a shoemaker; he stood just under six feet tall and was described as having several scars on his left hand and a scar on his left cheek. The decision in response to Ellen Lee's petition stated that his mother had given no grounds for changing the sentence, and therefore 'He had better go to Parkhurst.' John was sent from Newgate in April 1841 to the *Euryalus* – a hulk reserved for juvenile prisoners – then finally on to Parkhurst Prison in October 1841. At this point Parkhurst was reserved for juveniles who had been sentenced to transportation for colonial training in the form of reading, writing and some trade training. At Parkhurst he was described as being unable to read and write. In 1843 John was sent back to the hulks again. This time he was sent to the *York* hulk, and then transported on the *Anson*, both adult ships, to Van Diemen's Land. The *Anson* sailed from Plymouth in October 1843 and arrived in February 1844. John was only 15 years of age on arrival, and could both read and write by the time he arrived in the colony. Presumably he had learnt to do so while confined at Parkhurst and possibly received further instruction on the voyage over. The surgeon-superintendent on the voyage reported that John's conduct was 'good' and that he had committed no offences but he was not employed, the suggestion being that they were unable to find tasks for him on the voyage. The hulk officials, on the other hand, described John's behaviour as 'bad'.

John's first known location in Van Diemen's Land was Point Puer, the juvenile penal station (discussed in Chapter Three), from where he absconded in July 1844. He was given fourteen days' solitary confinement as a result. He was then found to be absent without leave in August 1844, and had his existing period of probation extended by six months. As a result of 'misconduct in making use of obscene language respecting the superintendent', he was given the punishment of thirty-six lashes. The following month he slipped his irons and was found sleeping with another man. This offence led to his existing sentence of hard labour being extended by another six months. It was further recommended that he be sent to a station where the separate system was in force, doubtless to prevent a similar offence occurring again. John was approximately 15 or 16 years old at this point. The implication is that there was inappropriate behaviour between him and another inmate, or the officials were afraid it would lead to this. What were contemporaneously termed 'unnatural acts' were illegal at this time. John then abused the watchman in the execution of his duties (probably answering back) and was given five days' solitary confinement.

John was convicted of a felony at Oatlands Supreme Court in April 1845. The *Colonial Times* reported that he was captured by a constable in Campbell Town. He was found guilty of assaulting Patrick Gillespie, putting him in 'bodily fear', and further stealing one pound. John, along with five others, was sentenced to be imprisoned with hard labour for three years, with two years of this sentence to be served at Port Arthur penal establishment.

In October 1845, while at Port Arthur, he used improper language (the usual bureaucratic term for obscene and threatening language), and was given fourteen days' hard labour. Later that month he was absent without leave and given a longer dose of hard labour, in chains this time. Then he disobeyed orders and neglected his duty again. His existing sentence of hard labour in chains was extended by another fourteen days. In September 1846 he was found smoking in his hut and given the punishment of one month's hard labour in chains. A month later, still in Port Arthur, he was found to have tobacco and buttons improperly in his possession and resisted the constable in the execution of his duty. This resulted in thirty-six lashes.

None of these punishments seemed to have had the slightest effect on him. After laughing and talking during divine service, he was given a further one month's hard labour in chains. He was given the same punishment yet again for 'holding communications contrary to orders' (talking to other inmates when he shouldn't have been). After an episode of insolence and attempting to strike his overseer, he was given the same punishment again but this time for a period of two weeks. Because he had bread improperly in his possession (stolen), he had his existing sentence of hard labour in chains extended by one month. Then he assaulted his overseer (prison guard) and was given thirty days' solitary confinement.

John then absconded. Upon recapture he was punished with fourteen days' solitary confinement, and then he had an extension of his probation sentence by six months because he was absent without leave. Using obscene language resulted in thirty-six lashes. Then he was absent without leave again in October and was given six months' hard labour, while disobedience of orders resulted in his existing sentence to hard labour in chains being extended by fourteen days.

It is clear to see, from John Lee's case here and also John Press's case, that being confined to a penal settlement such as Port Arthur resulted in a large number of offences committed while 'under sentence'. This is likely a reflection of the increased surveillance and strict regulations of the penal settlement compared with being assigned to a free settler.

John was free by April 1848 and living in New Norfolk. However, he was caught stealing a pair of boots just three months later. This resulted in two months' hard labour. The following month John absconded and was given twelve months' imprisonment and hard labour in chains. He began this sentence at Turnbridge but was moved to Port Arthur and placed in separate treatment. In January 1849 he was found fighting but was only reprimanded. He was then charged with misconduct for refusing to take medicine and given three months' solitary confinement. Again, due to fighting in the works, he was given seven days' solitary confinement. Insolence resulted in his existing sentence of imprisonment and hard labour being extended by two months. Yet again he was found fighting, but this time in school, which resulted in seven days' solitary confinement. He received the same punishment in April 1850 for having a pipe of tobacco in his possession, contrary to orders. This latter offence was the last noted in his conduct record. He was free again by April 1850.

Like many ex-convicts, when free John made his way to Victoria. Gold had been discovered there in 1850 and many settlers were flocking there to make their fortune. In October 1853 John voyaged from Launceston as one of the steerage passengers on the *Clarence* heading for Melbourne. From this point, however, he disappears from the records, and we cannot find out whether he did, in fact, discover any gold or make a new life for himself in Melbourne.

7. John Press (b.1831)

Born in 1831, John Press was named after his father. He had a brother, William, and together they lived in Whitechapel, London. From a young age John was repeatedly before the courts. In April 1841 he was found guilty of simple larceny for stealing three half-crowns, nine shillings and three sixpences. Despite his professed young age, he had been convicted previously and was described as having been in the 'house of correction often'. He was there once for stealing a loaf of bread, for which he was given one month's confinement, and again for a similar offence he was given two months; he received another two months for picking a woman's pocket, and a further six weeks for another similar offence. Lastly, he received three months and an additional flogging for housebreaking.

John was only 10 years old when he was sentenced to transportation at the Old Bailey. While awaiting his voyage to Australia, John was kept on board the *Euryalus* hulk. This was a decommissioned warship moored at Chatham and used to house only juvenile male convicts. The hulk authorities reported that John was 'indifferent and artful', and later the surgeon-superintendent of his convict transport recorded that he was 'flogged and punished several times on board'. He was transported on board the *Lord Goderich*, leaving from Portsmouth in September 1841, and arrived in Hobart. In his Conduct Record the section which acts as a 'description' (created for authorities to distinguish him from other convicts and identify him if he escaped) described him as having two dots between his thumb and forefinger on his right hand, and a mole inside his left arm. John had learnt to read but could not write at his point. Despite his behaviour being recorded as bad, both in confinement and on the voyage over, thanks to his youth he was still immediately placed at Point Puer. This juvenile penal settlement adjacent to Port Arthur admitted only male juvenile convicts up to 20 years of age, with the average age being around 14.

John's first colonial offence did not occur until January 1844, when he was found to be absent without leave and was given five days' solitary confinement. At this point he was still only about 13 and was under probation. He had therefore behaved very well while stationed at Point Puer. He was granted a free certificate in April 1848 when his seven-year sentence expired. However, in February 1849 John committed an offence, stealing two bottles containing lemon essence and six jars of snuff from his master, Mr John Henry De La Hunt. He pleaded guilty and was re-transported for seven years, one year of which was to be hard labour. A news report by the *Colonial Times* stated that he had robbed Mr Hunt 'to a very great extent by abstracting medicines in small quantities at a time'.

Now at Port Arthur, which was a notorious penal settlement, John was no longer segregated from adult convicts. After all, he was now 18 years old and was on a sentence of re-transportation. Many offences followed. In 1849 John was reprimanded for disorderly conduct. When he tampered with his convict uniform he was given three days' solitary confinement. When he used improper language (swearing) he was given one month's imprisonment with hard labour (in chains). Then, because of misconduct in shouting and making a disturbance while in solitary confinement, he was given a further three months' imprisonment and hard labour in March 1850. He absconded in August of that year and was given twelve months' hard labour in chains. Disorderly conduct in his cell resulted in fourteen days' solitary confinement in November. When he became a pass holder the following year, he did not obey the conditions properly (he was out after curfew) and was given four days' solitary confinement. Passes were granted in the probation period allowing convicts to work and live freely in the colony but with certain conditions such as living in particular areas – usually out of the towns. Next, John was convicted of stealing property (valued at less than five pounds), and given an extended sentence of eighteen months' hard labour in chains. Shortly after, his reported idleness resulted in a further four months' hard labour extension. Then, he committed an offence that, in the eyes of the authorities, was even more heinous than his own idleness: he was endeavouring to incite men to neglect their work, which resulted in his sentence of hard labour being extended by a further two months. For misconduct in chapel during prayers he was given seven days' solitary confinement. More idleness in 1853 resulted in another seven days' solitary confinement. Next he ill-treated a fellow prisoner in June of the same year, and was given fourteen days' solitary confinement. In October 1854, at the age of 23, John was eventually granted his ticket of leave.

While John Press offended frequently and certainly committed a range of serious offences, he was also described as a 'good tailor' when stationed at Point Puer and was forwarded to New Town Farm for hiring without having committed *any* offences. It had become common practice to send juvenile convicts from Point Puer to New Town Farm once they were proficient in their trade. He therefore had become proficient in his trade and had behaved well up until this point. It was only when he was released that his offences began and he seemed to enter a downward spiral. He sought permission to marry Bridget Keady in November 1854, immediately after he was awarded his ticket of leave during his second sentence of transportation. It was approved and they married in a Roman Catholic church the following month. While John was Protestant, it is likely that, given the choice of church, the Irish-born Bridget was Catholic. They were both 25 when they married. They had two children: Mary Ann, who was born in Fingal when John was a labourer and died in 1928, and a son Joseph, who was born in Ross in 1854.

John did not appear before the courts again for over a decade but his offending career was not over. In 1867, aged 36, he was convicted at Launceston for stealing a horse worth two pounds from his workplace – Deloraine Tramway works – and given four years' imprisonment. John had been spotted with the horse, along with his wife, son and daughter. In his defence, he stated that he was lent the horse for one pound. John called on his son Joseph to testify. Joseph, who was only 12 years of age, was also committed to the gaol with his father on the same charge: 'the boy without being questioned delivered what appeared to be a made-up statement, to the effect that his father had paid Davidson £1 for the loan of the horse'. The *Cornwall Chronicle* reported that John Press was found guilty but Joseph was released on the condition his 'mother take control of him'. A further report by the *Launceston Examiner* described the statement given by Joseph as a 'rambling statement, which the little fellow had evidently got to memory'.

By December John absconded from a work gang in the Queen's Domain but was recaptured and consequently given nine months' hard labour on top of his sentence. By 1869 John was free again but was once more before the courts, along with his wife Bridget Press, aged 40, who was also free by servitude. Tried at the Supreme Court in Hobart Town, both were acquitted of stealing sheep. Other charges included stealing and receiving meat. The prisoners were defended in court but there was confusion over what could be said in their defence because they were arraigned on a joint charge. At this point

John was working for a butcher named William Bailey. The *Mercury* allows us a glimpse into the home life of this family, mentioning 'Mary Ann Press, the daughter of the prisoners, who deposed that her mother had run away from her father'. They were both found *not* guilty. Although they were not convicted, this article suggests there was discord within the family.

John's next court appearance was in Brighton in August 1873. John, Bridget and Mary Ann had broken into Joseph Ormond's house at Bagdad and stolen bread and beef. *The Tasmanian* newspaper stated that the police could not prove the breaking-in, and they were subsequently only found guilty of larceny. John received six months' hard labour, Bridget one month and Mary just one hour, presumably to scare her into desisting from crime. We don't know where Joseph was at this point. John was discharged from the house of correction by February 1874. Details of John Press's death cannot be located but it is evident that he had a turbulent life after he had earned his release into the colony.

8. Eliza White (1832–1847) and Elizabeth Jones *aka* Walford (1828–1905)

While some convicts transported in their youth lived long lives in the colony, such as Elizabeth Jones, who lived to the grand age of 74, others died young. Eliza White died soon after arrival.

Eliza was born in 1832 and was convicted in December 1845 of stealing two dustpans worth two shillings from a dwelling house in Lambeth. She was sentenced to be transported for seven years. She had been previously convicted of theft back in February of the same year. Her parents petitioned for mitigation on the grounds of her youth, and they promised that she would not offend again. However, there were no other signatures on their petition and they were unsuccessful. In May 1846 Eliza was transported on board the *Sea Queen* from Woolwich to Hobart. The surgeon-superintendent described her as 'Bad, Idle and dirty – sent to hospital' and unfortunately all other records were left blank. It was a relatively short journey for the convicts on this transport. Arriving at the end of August, Eliza unfortunately did not survive her first year in the colony. She died in June 1847 and was buried at the Prisoners Burial Ground at Trinity Cemetery.

Eliza had initially been sent to the *Anson* hulk for her six months' probation. The *Anson* was previously a warship but was refitted as a

NAME, *Whyte Eliza* No.

Trade ....
Height (without Shoes) ....
Age ....
Complexion ....
Head ....
Hair.................
Whiskers............
Visage ....
Forehead ....
Eyebrows............
Eyes ....
Nose................
Mouth ....
Chin................
Native Place.........
Marks ....

Eliza White's
Description List
(CON19-1-5)
(Available at LINC).

prison ship and moored at Prince of Wales Bay, Risdon, near Hobart. The *Anson* was used to house female convicts from 1844 (and was broken up in 1850) in an attempt to alleviate the overcrowding at the Cascades Female Factory (see Chapter Three).

The British government wanted to keep the punishment of transportation as cheap as possible, and as a result there were numerous complaints about the conditions for convicts during the voyages. Reluctance to make improvements on the grounds of economy led to inevitable overcrowding of the transports. Before the convicts were sent, the surgeon-superintendent decided, in theory, who was healthy enough to be transported. Any convict with an infectious disease or who was deemed unfit to travel was not supposed to be transported. The criteria for selection were also supposedly based on age: males under the age of 15 and older than 50, and females over 45 years of age were not to be transported. However, juveniles under the age of 15 were, in fact, transported.

After 1815 there was a surgeon-superintendent placed on every convict ship who was responsible for the health and discipline of the convicts on board. It was thanks to the surgeons' exertions for good hygiene that health improved on convict ships. These surgeon-superintendents were also responsible for picking the convicts who were fit to sail. However, naval surgeons complained about the impossibility of this task, pointing to the desire of the convicts to hide illness in order to get a place on the transport, as well as the practice of hulk authorities, keen to get rid of their more troublesome charges, of transporting them regardless of their condition – although of course this was denied. Certainly there is evidence of convicts gaining places on convict transports while suffering from ill health. Dishonesty may or may not have led to such circumstances but it does illustrate that, despite efforts to the contrary, some convicts were ill before they boarded the ship; this could not only lead to their own deaths, but might also spread diseases to other passengers.

The Admiralty took direct control over convict transportation in 1832, long before Eliza was transported. Prior to this, the vessels were chartered from private ship-owners. Conditions on the voyage did improve over the period of transportation from 1787 to 1868. Mortality was intolerably high from the 1790s to 1815. However, after improvements were introduced, the average death rate per voyage fell. When taken in context, the transportation of convicts was not exceptionally hazardous. The Royal Navy's estimate during the Napoleonic Wars was that one sailor in thirty would die of disease or accident. Moreover, the free emigrant ships to the United States in the mid-nineteenth century also saw a death rate of one in thirty. Convicts were different as they were sent against their will. Nevertheless, tragic cases like that of Eliza were not the norm. Many females transported as juvenile convicts lived well into old age.

* * *

Elizabeth Jones was convicted in 1842 for stealing from her master one shawl worth two shillings and two pence, one bonnet worth six pence, and three pence in change. At the Old Bailey she stated in her defence: 'You gave me the bonnet to wear, and lent me the shawl; you took me into your service at 1s. a week and my victuals [but] you never gave me a farthing of money, and scarcely any victuals.'

Despite her claims, Elizabeth was found guilty and sentenced to seven years' transportation. She sailed aboard the *Garland Grove* in October 1842, arriving in Hobart three months later. Once in the colony, Elizabeth committed only three offences (all non-serious, regulatory offences) while under assignment. These included being absent without leave, misconduct and disobeying orders. For the first two offences she received a period in solitary confinement but the last offence resulted in six months' hard labour at the wash tub. Elizabeth received her ticket of leave in November 1847 after less than three years in the colony. She received her conditional pardon in July 1848 and in May 1849 she was awarded her certificate of freedom.

Four years after becoming free, Elizabeth Jones married Henry Rowbottom. Henry was a tradesman who had been transported from London for seven years in 1844. In total they had four children between 1851 and 1858, three sons and a daughter. The eldest was born before they married. Elizabeth died in an invalid depot in Launceston aged 74 and was buried in February 1905 at Charles Street General Cemetery. Her husband Charles also died at the invalid depot, aged 77.

9. Hannah Mary Dowse (b.1833) and Pleasance Temperance Neale (b.1832)

Hannah Mary Dowse was born in April 1833 to Mary Ann and James Dowse, and was baptised in July 1833 at St John the Evangelist's Church in Smith Square, Middlesex. At the time, the family lived in Vincent Place and the father was working as a labourer. By the time Hannah was 13 years of age they were still living in London, but now in Marylebone. The household comprised Hannah's parents, James (aged 46 and now a rail porter) and her mother Mary (aged 44), as well as her older sibling James William Dowse (aged 20) and her younger sibling John Dowse (aged just 5), along with a lodger from Cork, Ireland, named J.S. Simmons.

Just four years later, when Hannah was 17, she was imprisoned in Newgate. During her trial, which took place at the Old Bailey in 1850, Hannah was accused of stealing a watch, a brooch, a guard and other unnamed articles to the value of two pounds and one pence. The goods belonged to her own brother James William Dowse, and he prosecuted her. At that time James was living in Portland Market. He said that on the evening of the offence he had hung up his watch on the mantelpiece and it was gone by morning. Their mother Mary Ann confirmed James's story. Hannah pleaded guilty to the charge and was sentenced to four months' imprisonment. Hannah, who was described as a spinster, had already pleaded guilty and therefore technically her mother was not speaking against her but was instead speaking against the co-defendant and for her son. However, Hannah had yet to be sentenced and her mother speaking for the prosecution was unlikely to have helped her case. Also on trial, accused of receiving the stolen goods, was Jane Martin. A policeman, John Pollard, stated that he had apprehended Jane Martin near her mother's house, where *her* own brother insisted 'You take this girl into custody for pawning a stolen watch.' He further asserted that at that time she confessed that she had pawned the watch and gave nineteen shillings and ten pence to Hannah. She was, nevertheless, found not guilty.

* * *

It was not uncommon for family members to prosecute children and juvenile-adults like Hannah. Another example, Pleasance Temperance Neale, was just 14 years of age when she was prosecuted at the Old Bailey by her own father in October 1847. Her father, who was then working as a servant, accused his daughter of stealing ten sovereigns from the dwelling house. Consequently, she was sentenced to twelve months' confinement. Pleasance pleaded guilty to this offence, just as Hannah had in her trial. Because she pleaded guilty, there is little information on the circumstances of this offence in the trial recording. It was only because Hannah's co-accused pleaded not guilty that we have the information surrounding the offence. It was often the case, when a family member was prosecuting, that juveniles pleaded guilty.

When Pleasance was 36 she was living in St Mary, Paddington, London, with her 74-year-old father and Elizabeth Oakes, his aged sister-in-law, and a lodger named Elizabeth Tindall (aged 24). At this time her father, originally from Norfolk Wells, was working as a coffee-house keeper and Pleasance was working as a waitress there while her aunt kept house. It would seem that after her stay in prison, life continued as normal and the family bonds were not severed. Similarly, while Hannah's relationship with her brother after her release from prison is unknown, she certainly reunited with her parents, and went on to marry William Pearce in Marylebone in June 1852 when she was 19 years of age. Her father was present at the wedding and is described as a porter; the bridegroom's father, also called William Pearce (a bricklayer), was also present. The bridegroom himself was a bricklayer, and at the time of the union they are both listed as living in Marylebone. Mary Ann Dowse, the mother who spoke for the prosecution in her trial, was also present as a witness. There is no evidence that either of these women committed further crimes after their confinement in prison, and they both sub-sequently disappear from the records after re-entering their respective families.

10. Horatio Nelson Branch (b.1836)

Horatio Nelson Branch was born in 1836. At the age of 12 he was placed at the Royal Philanthropic School. Established in London in 1788 (and closed in 1906), the Philanthropic Society was concerned with the care of homeless children left to fend for themselves by begging or thieving. Those admitted to the school were either the children of criminals, or those who had been convicted of crimes themselves but were particularly young – as in the case of Horatio. The school was eventually moved to Redhill in 1849 to begin its farm school training based on the French reform school Mettray (see Chapter Three). As Horatio was sent to the school rather than to Parkhurst, this suggests that his case was seen as hopeful and that he was considered to be reformable. After 1847 the increasingly penal establishment of Parkhurst was reserved for juveniles over 14 years of age, whereas the younger, more promising cases were kept in the reform school.

By 13 years of age Horatio was working as a labourer. He was convicted at this time for stealing seven sovereigns and two half sovereigns from Elizabeth Branch, his mistress. Horatio pleaded guilty and was given fourteen days' solitary confinement at Newgate; on top of this he was also whipped. Sir John Eardley-Wilmot, as High Sheriff of Warwickshire, had worked on the Warwick County Asylum for Juvenile Offenders (which had opened in 1818 and was the first reformatory outside London). In this position, he wrote a letter to the magistrates about the 'Increase of Crime' in 1827, advocating the summary whipping of juveniles, the intention being that juveniles would be given a short, sharp shock to deter them from crime. However, in Horatio's case he was also imprisoned, thus – in contemporary views – contaminating him through mixing with adult offenders. Horatio's whipping would have taken place in private. Public whipping had declined for men as early as the 1830s. Despite considerable opposition to the flogging of adults, often those same individuals did not oppose flogging the young. Many in authority did not feel that the degrading effect flogging had on adults extended to juveniles. This was largely because the physical punishment of the young was, by tradition, a well established method of child discipline. Flogging for adult men was seen by many as a last resort, but for male juveniles it was placed at the other end of the scale. The idea was that a 'short, sharp punishment' was better than long periods of imprisonment for the young. Indeed, it was not until 1920 that a Home Office report concluded that corporal punishment of juveniles was largely ineffective as a means of deterring youths from reoffending, although it remained in widespread use for boys, rising significantly during the two world wars, until the passage of the Criminal Justice Act in 1948.

Horatio next appears in the records in the Old Bailey in August 1849. This time he stood accused of embezzlement and stealing fifteen shillings from his master, Samuel Hartley. This was a more serious offence. He again pleaded guilty and was confined for six months. He was later convicted again for stealing two half-crowns, seven shillings and one sixpence from Frederick Davidge. At his trial he also admitted to having previous offences and consequently was confined for twelve months. In September 1850 he was charged with fraud but 'no bill' was found (the case was therefore thrown out at a preliminary stage).

In February 1852, when he was approximately 16 years old, Horatio emigrated to Australia on board the *Arrogant* from Redhill. It is unclear how Horatio had ended up at Redhill at this time but after 1849 the Philanthropic Society would, at the end of some of the juveniles' terms, provide boys with a set of clothing and arrange the details of passage for them to a British colony. This applied to those predestined to emigration, but Redhill also continued to train boys (known as 'Government Account' boys) who were transferred from the London prison. It is likely that Horatio was among the latter. He arrived in Australia as a free man, not as a convict.

The Surrey History Centre has an online index of the boys who were in the Royal Philanthropic Society home between 1788 and 1906. In this index information on Horatio can be found. The whole collection comprises the surviving records of the Society and its school all the way up until 1997, when it merged with the Rainer Foundation (with obvious access restrictions). It includes, for example, Annual Reports (1848–1976, with some gaps), General Court and General Committee Minutes (1793–1937), Finance Committee Reports (1856–1914), Journals (1793–1848, 1896–1933, 1946–1963), photographs (c.1891–c.1970) and Registers of Admissions (1788–1967).

Horatio arrived in Port Phillip, Victoria, in April 1853 when he was still only 17 years old. He was described as an English labourer

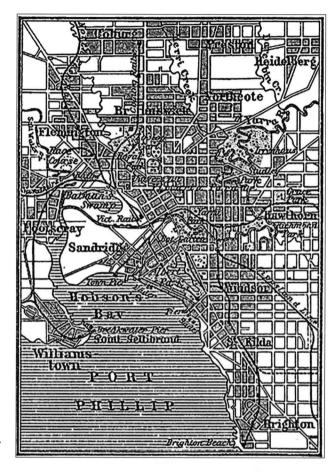

Port Phillip, Victoria.
(*Wikimedia Commons*)

in the Victoria Inward Passenger Lists (1839–1923). It is likely that he emigrated to Australia in order to make his fortune or simply to earn his livelihood. Horatio went on to marry, in September 1864, Jessie Wilson in Queensland, Australia.

11. Ann Gill (b.1842)

Ann Gill was born in Yorkshire, in the parish of St Luke's, in 1842, where she was raised a Protestant. Ann had green eyes, brown hair and grew to five feet and two and a quarter inches. When Ann was just 11 years of age she was brought before the Middlesex Sessions (which dealt with more serious offenders) and was found guilty of stealing a pair of boots. She was sentenced to two months' imprisonment. A year later she was convicted of stealing twenty-two yards of cloth at Clerkenwell. This time, aged 13, she was sentenced to four months' imprisonment. In 1859, now 17, Ann was convicted of 'stealing from the person'.

At this time it was reported that she was in good health but she could neither read nor write. Her father was Patrick Flynn, who lived at 3 Stable Court, Rope Maker Street, Finsbury. In 1859 she was confined in Westminster House of Correction. By 1862 she had been moved to Fulham Prison. The Director General of Convict Prisons, Sir Joshua Jebb, was instrumental in developing Fulham Prison, so much so in fact that the inmates were known as 'Jebb's pets'. The prison trained the 400 female inmates in laundry duties, and that may have helped Ann to gain a job as a laundrywoman when she was released. It might also have given her the opportunity to get into more trouble, though.

In June 1864, now aged 22, Ann was found guilty of simple larceny, along with Elizabeth Welland (aged 21) and Fanny Barrett (aged 18), for stealing forty yards of cloth, the property of George Hawkesley. While Fanny was sentenced to be confined for one year, due to their previous convictions Ann and Elizabeth were given the much heavier punishment of seven years' penal servitude.

At this time Ann was unmarried and unemployed. In July she was transferred to Millbank Prison where she was employed as a picker and her behaviour is recorded as good. At this time she was kept in separate confinement and her progress in the prison school (where she would have to pass reading and writing tests in order to gain better conditions inside the prison) was satisfactory. In October she was sent to Brixton Prison, where her behaviour was still reported as good and she was now employed in needlework and her progress in school was 'tolerable'. In April 1868 Ann was sentenced to be in her cell all day as punishment for having a bottle in her possession. The following month Ann was transferred back to Fulham Prison and was occupied again in the laundry. Her conduct was reported as 'very good'. That April, Ann was granted conditional freedom on a licence; she was now 26 years of age and living in a Fulham refuge, but in July 1868 she was punished for striking another prisoner. In August she was transferred to Battery House in Winchester and by December she was at Millbank, where she received medical attention. Unfortunately, the exact details of her health and treatment are not recorded in her prison record. Ann was finally granted her conditional licence to 'be at large' in May 1870 and was discharged from prison as a 'habitual criminal'.

The Habitual Criminal Registers were established following the 1871 Prevention of Crimes Act, which gave police the power to supervise and apprehend repeat offenders and those designated 'habitual criminals' like Ann. The registers were created as a means of supervising habitual criminals, with details of individuals being circulated around different police forces. A database of more than 100,000 habitual criminals was kept by the Metropolitan Police in England and Wales between 1881 and 1925. Ann was recorded in the registers under the name 'Hinchliffe' in 1882. Information on individuals who had been convicted of more than two offences were collected by the police to help with both surveillance and future identification of known offenders. By this time Ann was only 28 years of age, and had grey hair. She had been working as a charwoman (a cleaner). We also know that she was a widow. Unfortunately, we do not have any information about her marriage, whether it produced any children or not, or the death of her husband (who, given the alias she used in the Habitual Offenders Registers, may have been called Hinchcliffe). With people like Ann, it is often the case that the lack of information throws up a whole raft of interesting questions.

12. Anthony Kehoe (1844–c.1901)

Anthony was born in Birkenhead in 1844, just as the industry that would later come to dominate that working-class town was getting under way. William Laird and Son established an iron works and shipbuilding yards which were thriving by the 1840s. The business which eventually became Cammell Laird came to be synonymous with the history of Birkenhead. The town was tough, and the family that Anthony was born into was tough as well.

Aged 14, Anthony was convicted of theft, whipped, and was then imprisoned for three months. The following year he stole some nails in Chester and was sent to reform school, but this did not stop his offending. When he was released he stole a pair of boots. Stealing boots was a crime born of poverty, and Anthony's life seems to have been quite desperate. When he was sentenced to three years' penal servitude in 1861 for taking the boots, the newspaper report stated that Anthony's father was 'King of Albion Street . . . assaulting his son and pitching into the bobbies . . .'. Perhaps Anthony was better off in prison than in his family home. He certainly spent a lot of time inside prison over the next few years. He was sent to Chester Castle Prison in 1864 for attempting to break into a shop at Birkenhead. Discharged at Birkenhead, he was imprisoned again for stealing money and yet again for being a rogue and a vagabond in Liverpool.

Up until this point, Anthony was a young thief, stealing to live and just about getting by, but in December 1864 his offending escalated. He was convicted of robbery with violence at Birkenhead: 'An incorrigible thief – a youth who had been only just released from Chester Castle ... the Prisoner knocked the victim down, kicked him in the mouth and rolled him in the mud ... This was the ninth time the prisoner had been before the court.' Anthony's brother John was also imprisoned for four months at Chester Quarter Sessions for a different offence: a 'garrotting' robbery (putting a knotted rope around the victim's throat and strangling them until they lost consciousness). This seemed like a pattern. The following year, after Anthony had served his prison sentence, he was again convicted for knocking down and robbing a drunk man late at night.

At this time Anthony may have been home on leave, for he had joined the Navy, which provided a good alibi in July 1865 when he was charged with assault and robbery at Birkenhead. The case was discharged as he proved that he was doing duty on HMS *Donegal* at Holyhead at the time of the offence. His solicitor stated that 'it was a case of mistaken identity; the prisoner's brother was very like the prisoner in personal appearance, and he had disappeared'. Anthony's luck ran out shortly afterwards, however. In November 1865 he was convicted of receiving stolen property and was sentenced to seven years' imprisonment.

After his release in 1871, he was involved in a violent fight in which a policeman's head was 'cut to the bone by a kick'. He received another year inside for that offence, and another ten years for theft of money in 1874. By his fortieth birthday he had spent more than half of his life in prison. Described now as an 'old offender', he would be convicted many more times, and spend many more years in prison. When he was out of prison, he voluntarily admitted himself to the local workhouse, which at least provided hot food and a bed. Anthony, hardened by prison life, could cope easily with harsh workhouse conditions.

By 1889 Anthony was revolving between prison, the workhouse and the workhouse hospital. He was stealing money to pay for drink, and to feed and clothe himself (once he stole the police superintendent's coat while reporting at Birkenhead police station). In 1892 he stole a bag at Birkenhead, accompanied by a friend (he was associating with many known offenders at this time). 'His lordship, in passing sentence, said that between them the prisoners had spent forty-nine years in penal servitude. What to do with such men as the prisoners he did not know. He was, however, going to surprise them with the sentences. He sentenced the prisoners to six months' hard labour' (*Liverpool Mercury*, 5 December 1892).

In 1895 Anthony racked up his thirty-second conviction, one which was out of character with his usual offending. He was convicted of an 'unnatural offence' (the usual term for a homosexual act) with a 21-year-old labourer at Birkenhead. He was sentenced to eighteen months' hard labour at Chester Assizes. Back in Birkenhead after his release, he committed his last offence, the theft of a leg of mutton from Birkenhead market. Sentenced to nine months at Birkenhead Sessions, he 'urged that he had been persecuted by the police and others, and also that he was in drink at the time of the offence, and consequently did not know what he was doing'. This was not a sufficiently rigorous or well-argued defence to get him off. He was again sent to prison, this time for nine months. In 1901 he was resident in Tranmere workhouse (in Cheshire, near Birkenhead), and finally disappears from the criminal records. Given the scale and frequency of his offending, it seems unlikely that he simply stopped and 'stayed on the straight and narrow'. It is much more likely that he died around this time.

Anthony had endured a hard and brutal life, which had left marks on his body. His prison record revealed the true extent. He had cuts and scars on his nose, over his eyebrows and on his forehead, two scars on his back and left shoulder, broken fingers, a missing right forefinger, and a number of prison tattoos (dots between his finger and thumb indicating that he had been a reformatory school boy). The mental scars from a violent upbringing, months spent in solitary confinement, years of imprisonment and a significant amount of time spent on the streets or in the workhouse were harder to document, but were no doubt there nevertheless.

13. Stanley Charles Selway *aka* Sillivay (1844–1927)

Stanley Charles Selway is known to have committed only one offence throughout his life. Born in 1844, Stanley was tried in May 1859 at the

Old Bailey, when he was 15 years of age, for the violent robbery of Charles Dear. He had stolen from him one box, valued at two shillings, and one pound, five shillings and three pence in money. During the course of the robbery Charles Dear had been 'struck and beat'. He was tried alongside his brother Samuel William Selway, 16 years of age, and James Wynne, 17 years of age. Samuel was found not guilty, whereas Stanley and Wynne were found guilty. Wynne was sentenced to ten years' penal servitude. Had it not been for a good character reference, it is likely Stanley could have received the same long sentence. However, Frederick Merdon, a clerk living in Cannon Street, and George Mallow, a boot-maker living in Goswell Street, both gave Stanley a good character. In the end he was given four years' penal servitude.

The prosecutor, Charles Dear, was a picture frame dealer in Essex Street. Stanley had been in his service as an errand boy for three weeks and was under notice to quit the following Sunday. In the trial transcript the prosecutor described the robbery and how the boys whistled to each other as a signal. Describing the event as a planned affair, Dear explained that Stanley was in the shop with him, working, when he whistled to his brother, Dear believed, as a signal. Then James Wynne (a stranger to the prosecutor but a friend of Stanley's) went into the shop and spoke to Stanley. Shortly after, Stanley forced open the cupboard and took out the cashbox, then Wynne hit Charles Dear on the back of the head with what he thought was a crow-bar. When Stanley ran away, with the cash box in his hand, he bumped into his brother in the street. It was because of this interaction that Samuel Selway was implicated, and was accused of colluding in the offence.

Stanley was sent to Parkhurst prison. By this point Parkhurst had become increasingly penal in nature and was considered by some as simply a prison for boys, rather than having the reformatory zeal it began with. Aged 15, Stanley was described as being five feet and four inches tall, with a freckled face, and having lived, prior to his conviction, in Doctors Commons. His brother Samuel was living in Camberwell, had a scar on his upper lip and was also freckled and was two inches taller. Stanley's next of kin is given as Mrs Selway (his mother) who was living at Hosier Lane, West Smithfield. Other documentation also described Stanley as being from Hozier Lane, where his mother then resided. There is no mention of his father.

A cell and galleries at Newgate Prison, from *The Queen's London* (1896).
(*Wikimedia Commons*)

Initially Stanley was sent from Newgate to Millbank Prison in June 1859, and so too was his accomplice James Wynne. When Stanley was received at Newgate, awaiting his trial, he could read and write only improperly. Next he was sent from Millbank to Parkhurst Prison in August 1859. He was described as having a fair complexion with a freckled face, brown hair and hazel eyes, and slender build. He was in good health and was a Protestant with no previous convictions. During his twenty-five days at Newgate, where he was kept in separate confinement, his behaviour was described as good. While at Millbank, Stanley also behaved well and was given the trade of tailor but in his two months and two days there he made no scholastic progress. However, during his four months at Parkhurst, while in separate confinement, his character is again described as good and his progress in school is also described as good. In Parkhurst, when moved to work on the Public Works, he was in association (which meant he was not kept solitary away from other prisoners). This is where he spent the bulk of his sentence, just over thirty-one months. Yet again he was given a good character and his progress was described as very satisfactory in school, and he had been working as a bookbinder. Through exploring the prison registers we can therefore trace Stanley as he was moved through the prison system.

107

Stanley was discharged on licence in August 1862. His destination on his release was Kings Street, Snow Hill, London. Now 18 years of age, he was described as being a labourer by trade. When he was convicted he had been an errand boy, and in prison he had been put to work in the trades of tailoring and bookbinding, but in what capacity we do not know. In search of work upon release Stanley joined the Scots Guards in May 1865 when he was 21 years of age. Standing just over five feet nine inches tall, with a fresh face, he described himself as a tailor from the parish of Walworth, London, Surrey. He became a lance corporal in the 61st (South Gloucestershire) Regiment of Foot and was discharged in 1873 when he was listed among the Chelsea Pensions in the British Army Service Records. The cause of this discharge was 'varicose veins', which were first noticed in Bermuda in 1870. They were caused by lifting heavy weights in the military stores. It was recorded that his 'injuries may be permanent but will not stop him working as a tailor'. When discharged from service he had been at Belfast (in March 1873), when he was 28 years and 10 months old. He was described as 5 feet and 10 inches tall. He had served for seven years and eighteen days in Canada and Bermuda. Although now unfit for further service, his conduct was described as very good and he was even given a good conduct badge. However, his name appears twice in the regimental defaulters' book and he was once tried by court martial. He was at this time intending to move back to London upon discharge.

Once his army days were behind him, Stanley went on to marry Catherine Gifford in 1874 in London. In the 1881 census he is listed as a licensed victualler living in Farwig Lane, Bromley, Kent, with his wife Catherine, who was 36 years old, from Bath, and also a licensed victualler. Stanley had two children, a daughter named Rose Lilian and her younger brother Charles S.W. Selway. They were able to afford to have two servants living with them in 1881, Jessie Castleton, a barmaid aged 17, and Annie Lee, a local girl of 14 who was working as a domestic servant. By 1891, when Stanley was 47 years of age, he was working as a tailor, a trade he learnt in prison, from his home in Penge Cottages, Croydon, Surrey, where he lived with his wife and two children. His daughter, by then aged 15, was working as a board school pupil teacher, and Charles was working at a business agent's office. In 1911 Stanley was still working as a tailor and his daughter, now 35, was a council school teacher; they were all still living together in Surrey. Stanley's son Charles later followed in his footsteps and joined the army, serving in the 38th Division South West Borders Regiment. In 1897 Stanley was still living in Penge Lane. He died aged 83 in Croydon in 1927 having committed only one offence through his whole life.

14. James Bradley (b.1853) and William Brown (b.1853)

In 1861 8-year-old James Bradley and his friend Peter Barrett were convicted of murdering 2-year-old George Burgess, a child they had never seen before that day. On the day in question they stripped their victim on a piece of waste ground near Stockport, took him to a nearby brook, and then forced him into the water head-first. They then took turns to beat him around the head and legs. When he was dead, they left the body there to be discovered the following day. When they were questioned by a police officer, they seemed distant and unconcerned with their predicament. At their trial at Chester Assizes they were represented by a skilled solicitor who implored the jury to bring in a verdict of manslaughter rather than murder on the grounds that the boys did not act with malice. The jury agreed, and the judge passed sentence.

Murder was a capital crime, but by the time Bradley and Barrett were sentenced, children were not sent to the gallows (see Chapter Three). Instead they were sent to one of a number of reformatories that had been established throughout England and Wales from the 1850s and 1860s. As described in Chapter Three, boys sentenced to spend time in a reformatory school at this time were first required to spend one month in prison, after which they were removed to a reformatory. Barratt and Bradley were ordered to stay in Bradwall Reformatory in Cheshire. Records of the reformatory kept at the National Archives reveal that Bradley could neither read nor write, had no previous convictions, his parents were Stockport hat-makers and he had two siblings.

Despite the opposition of the Home Secretary, he was discharged on conditional licence in 1866 under the authority of George Latham, founder and manager of Bradwall Reformatory. The regime in his institution was strict, but allowed for privileges to be progressively earned (the progress of each child was recorded) and the institution was praised by HM Inspectors of Reformatory Schools for their success. Indeed, Latham and his successors received many letters of thanks from ex-inmates, such as these two which can be found in *Young Criminal Lives* (2017).

I write these few lines hoping you are well, as it leaves me at present. I hope the boys had a Merry Xmas this year, which no doubt they did judging by my own experience. I do not know if you heard that I have not been well. I was nearly going into a rapid consumption ... I think without boasting that you have made a man of me and I am glad I was corrected when I was. I can imagine you reading these reports of the boys out so I thought I would tell you how much I have benefited by your advice and instructions. Give my best respects to the Officers as I think very highly of them, and also W. Wellesby, the schoolmaster. Would you kindly let me know the address of William Webb and whether he has done well. My Aunt wishes to be remembered to you, also my Grandfather. I will be coming to see you on about Good Friday if all is well ... Willie Adams seems to be doing well in the Furniture Trade, but I do not have much to do with him, so I will close my letter hoping to hear from you.

I hope the letter finds you and the Matron and the family quite well. I hope W. Wellesby has got a good boy in the schoolroom. I should like to know how Rhodes (Toad) and Cross and a few more of the lower class boys are all getting on as I always took an interest in the lower classes. You will be sorry to hear that Jimmy Colburst has turned out very lazy, he has only done a few weeks work since he left Bradwall. I am sure I shall never forget being in Bradwall, it has learnt me not to be afraid of hard work, and there is plenty of that here, therefore I hope that the boys of Bradwall will take an interest in their work and remember what good advice you give to them and take notice of it, and above all not to shirk their work, as I have found out the benefits that can be got by sticking to your task till it is finished, though I often get jeered at it by a few of the idle set but I take no notice of it, they will see who has the laugh in the end.

Bradley never returned to Stockport and it is likely that he emigrated (according to investigative journalist Gita Sereny in the *Independent*, 23 April 1995).

*   *   *

Fifty years later fellow Bradwall boy William James Brown also emigrated to Canada. He was sent to the reformatory in 1901 for three years. During his time in Bradwall he joined the band (musical lessons were part of the regime) and learned to play the cornet. After leaving the reformatory, he enlisted as a 'band boy' with Winston Churchill's regiment, the 21st Lancers but left a year later. His character was recorded as 'very good' by his regiment, so it seems that he simply wanted to try a different career, rather than being dismissed. In fact, he picked up a number of temporary jobs (working variously as a barman, mechanic, chauffeur and waiter).

The census shows that by 1911 he had found his feet and started work as a photographer's assistant in London. Due to his failing health, he left for Ontario, Canada, and again managed to pick up a job as a photographer. During this time he continued to send letters back to the Bradwall staff. Commenting on the regular reports and photographs he sent back to Stockport, they called him 'a fine young man, quite a swell'. Like Bradley, he never reoffended. Thirty years after he left Bradwall, William and his wife visited the school. Most of the staff who had been at Bradwall would have left or died by that date, but it is a very strong indication of the affection that some ex-reformatory children had for their former institution, and a sign of the pride that some men felt at having made it through to a successful life in the end.

15. Thomas Priest (1854–1890)

Thomas lived with his parents and brothers and sisters in a working-class district of Sheffield. At 12 years old he may have followed his father into the spring-making business, or one of the other steel-related employment options that occupied most of the male population of Sheffield. However, on 19 April 1865 he was prosecuted for stealing money under the Juvenile Offenders Act (see Chapter Two) and sent to prison for a month. The experience does not seem to have had much impact on him. He was prosecuted again under the Juvenile Offenders Act in July, this time for stealing from someone's garden. He was sentenced to two months' imprisonment, but the magistrates also thought he needed closer supervision and so sent him to a reformatory for five years.

Almost as soon as he left the reformatory, he was convicted of theft (of twelve hens) and on 1 April at Wakefield Quarter Sessions he was sentenced to a year in prison. Again the judges felt he needed supervision. Because he had been convicted of two indictable (more serious) offences, he was eligible to be sentenced to a period of police supervision under the habitual offenders' acts.

Since the 1860s there were attempts to keep a watchful eye over released convicts, at least for the period they were released on licence. The 1869 Habitual Offender Act and the Prevention of Crime Act of 1871 (together known as the Habitual Offenders Acts) extended this power by giving the sentencing judge the power to order a set period of police supervision for offenders who had committed two or more indictable offences, as Thomas had done. On release from prison, supervisees were required to report to the police, and inform them every fortnight of where they were residing. If any person under supervision reoffended, consorted with thieves and prostitutes, or could not prove they were making an honest living, they could be imprisoned for up to a year. The judges decided on seven years' police supervision for Thomas. He would have to watch his step.

Thomas was now an 18-year-old young man who had served three terms of imprisonment and every police constable in Sheffield was minded to stop and search him whenever they saw him to check whether he was behaving himself. Not surprisingly, he was convicted of a number of minor offences over the next few years. He didn't really help himself, though. In February 1872 he stole six ginger-pop bottles from the doorstep of Sheffield magistrates court, for which he was fined twenty shillings and court costs. A few months later he was stopped by a police officer as he appeared to be drunk whilst riding a horse. The man who was riding with him ended up in prison for assaulting the police officer who was trying to arrest Thomas.

As an ex-prisoner, Thomas probably found good employment hard to come by. He and his brother Henry managed to get jobs carting horse manure around town in 1872, and in 1873 they were both in court for causing their horse to suffer an injury (two bad saddle-sores, which were caused by not changing the saddle often enough). They were convicted of animal cruelty and fined ten shillings.

In 1875 Thomas, Henry and some of their friends ended up in Doncaster. They were blind drunk, having broken into a store of alcohol. They were chased by the police and by some of the local militia. (The militia was comprised of local men who were volunteer soldiers, called up when there was a threat to law and order.) Thomas and his drunk mates did not constitute that sort of threat but the militiamen were probably drilling and practising in the neighbourhood and heard the commotion. Thomas gave a false name when he was arrested, but his true identity was soon discovered. The magistrates sent him to prison for two months for the theft of alcohol, and another month for assaulting one of the militiaman.

Thomas did not seem to be very good at learning lessons in life. In October 1875 he was again fined for cruelty to a horse (over-whipping the poor animal). This time the prosecuting agency was not the police, but the RSPCA, which was legally entitled to act as prosecutor – and did so numerous times. The twenty-shilling fine Thomas received for this offence was added to the ten-shilling fine he received the following day for having turned up to court to face the animal cruelty charge completely blind drunk.

Possibly because the period of police supervision had now passed, Thomas did not reappear in court for a few years. However, in 1879 he was back in Sheffield magistrates court, charged with stealing the watch of a man who had taken him in when he had nowhere else to sleep. The presiding magistrate was astounded that Thomas had repaid his good Samaritan in this way. How could he steal from a man who had been kind to him? Unabashed, Thomas replied that 'if he had the chance, he would do it again'. He was sent to Wakefield Prison for six months to consider whether this was a wise reply.

In 1881 Thomas received another twelve months in prison for stealing a pony. By this time he had thirteen previous convictions, and was probably considered to be at least a nuisance and possibly a habitual career criminal by the judges and magistrates of South Yorkshire. In 1883 he was charged with stealing eight pigeons and, because of his ever-growing list of previous convictions, he was dealt with at Sheffield Assizes. Although it was a low-value theft, he was sentenced to five years' penal servitude in a convict prison.

Thomas served most of his sentence in Pentonville in London, and he infringed the prison rules on many occasions during that time, including using improper language to a prison officer, assaulting fellow prisoners and 'wrangling' (quarrelling) with both officers and other prisoners. In convict prisons the inmates could earn 'marks' through prison labour, and lose 'marks' when they breached the regulations. Thomas progressed well enough in prison to be eligible for early release, and he was discharged to return to Sheffield, with eleven months of his sentence not served, on 14 May 1887. Three years later Thomas died. He was just 37 years old.

Thomas's life was made difficult after he had been in reformatory for five years (yet many reformatory school children did go on to

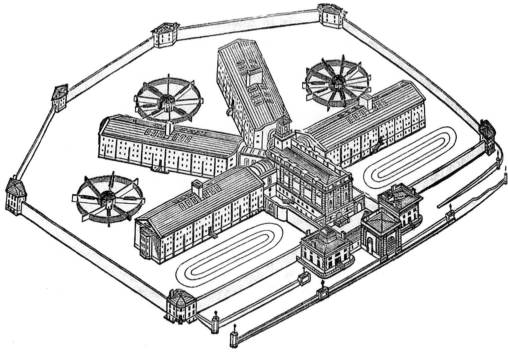

Isometrical perspective of Pentonville Prison, 1840–1842, engineer Joshua Jebb. Report of the Surveyor-General of Prisons, London, 1844. Image reproduced in Mayhew, *Criminal Prisons of London* (London, 1862). (*Wikimedia Commons*)

have successful lives, see Chapter Three). Perhaps Thomas might have gone on to lead a better life if he had not got into trouble almost as soon as he left the reformatory. If he had gained a job, maybe settled down with a wife, and had children, he would have had a different type of life. As it was, he was able to keep up relationships with his brother and he managed to have a rumbustious alcohol-fuelled life which he may have enjoyed very much until his early and untimely death (the reason for his death is unknown to us).

16. Joseph Tomlinson (1860–1920)

Joseph appears in lots of institutional records, but is still somewhat hard to trace because he is recorded under different names. No doubt the police would see these as aliases designed to help him avoid detection and identification, and perhaps they were, but they are just as likely to be nicknames (i.e. he is known as 'Chalky' for some reason). In 1860, though, he was called Joseph when he was born in

Crewe to father George, a general labourer, and mother Elia. He was, and remained, their only child.

In 1871 he was sent to Bradwall reformatory for an unspecified offence and remained there until he was 14 (like other parents, his father was brought to court for failing to pay the parental contribution to the reform school). He was back in reform school in 1874 when he stole a jacket from a local shop and pawned it. As with the Artful Dodger (see Chapter Two), he was considered to be 'a precocious lad' with adult characteristics. But worse was to come for Joseph when he did actually become an adult.

After serving a month in prison and four more years in the reform school, he started an apprenticeship at Crewe Railway Works in 1879, a job arranged for him by the reform school staff, but he was quickly sacked for not working hard enough, and then was convicted of two thefts in 1880. The first, in May, earned him a three-month custodial sentence; the second, in November, concerned theft of property of around the same value. This one, however, was considered to be a theft 'after previous conviction' and therefore he became subject to a five-year sentence of penal servitude in Pentonville prison. In 1883 he was released on conditional licence and he seems to have kept out of trouble for four years.

A casual theft of some calf-skin from a market stall earned him another few months in prison. Then in 1890 he was convicted of a serious offence: housebreaking. A single young man, working off and on as a labourer, who was 'well known to the police', he was always going to 'go away' for a considerable period of time. He was sent to Knutsford prison in Cheshire until 1895. This is the first time we have an assessment of his character. The newspaper report stated that he was 'a simple fellow'. He was, however, a rather more complex character than that comment suggests.

Joseph was convicted of assaulting John Leigh in 1896, and of being drunk in the Castle Hotel and refusing to leave the following year. These offences were minor compared to the offence he committed in 1897. The single young iron-moulder lodging in Crewe, and already known as a 'bad character', was sentenced to ten years' imprisonment for the rape of an 11-year-old girl in Crewe (although we know the name of his young victim, we prefer not to name her – see Chapter Four).

Whilst Joseph was in prison, both of his parents died. He walked out through the prison gates in 1903 a vagrant, unemployed young man, very much on his own. But, as a newspaper report of 1903 made clear, he could also attract a crowd: 'There were about 100 boys collected around the prisoner. There have been numerous complaints about Tomlinson and Joseph Briggs assembling on the market ground on Sunday afternoons. Tomlinson had a terrible record.' Joseph and his new friend had been shouting swear words towards a funeral procession before the police arrested them.

Again, Joseph seems to have committed many small thefts or nuisances alongside very serious offences. Some of the offences, such as worrying the grieving funeral-attenders, appeared to be 'stupid' and nonsensical. We can begin to see why the newspaper referred to him as 'a simple man'. Now called James Tomlinson, he was in the newspapers again later in 1903 for breaching the terms of his early release:

'Serious charge against a ticket-of-leave man – James Tomlinson, neglecting to report under ticket-of-leave.' In 1897 he had been sentenced to penal servitude for an assault on a child. At the beginning of the present year he had been liberated from Dartmoor and had reported regularly to the police until recently, when he disappeared. He was traced to Sandbach where he was living with a girl under the age of 16, an imbecile. The prisoner said he meant to marry her, and that the banns were being arranged. The girl's mother had given information to the police. He received two months for his disgraceful behaviour.

Tomlinson's behaviour was deteriorating, and he was becoming fixed on a series of sexual offences. He was convicted of an indecent assault on an 8-year-old boy in 1904. 'Tomlinson has a terrible record', reported the press. He then committed an indecent assault in 1907 on a 7-year-old girl, and in 1910 was charged with having unlawful carnal knowledge of a 13-year-old girl called Florence, and unlawful carnal knowledge of a 12-year-old boy (unlawful carnal knowledge was used as a euphemism for a number of sex acts, including homosexuality). The report in the *Crewe Chronicle* (29 April 1911) (again we have anonymised the names of the victims) was remarkable:

'Florence Roberts (referred to as Florence Harbridge) beyond the control of her parents.' Mrs Alice Roberts of Naylor Street made an application for her daughter Florence Harbridge aged 14 to be sent away, as she was quite beyond her control. The mother related a remarkable story of her daughter's behaviour, which the Bench said they could hardly have believed. Supt Pearson said that some time back a man named Tomlinson was sent to ten years' penal servitude, and a further two years' imprisonment, for a serious offence in which this particular girl was concerned. PC Darrall said he had watched the girl's house, but had not been able to make an arrest. Inspector Robinson, NSPCC, said that the girl's mother was a hard-working woman. She had five children. Her husband had deserted her, and she had to go out charring in order to keep the home together. It was whilst she was away that the girl's behaviour was very bad. The neighbours had given the girl a very bad name. In reply to Supt Pearson, witness said the girl was not of weak intellect.

Tomlinson was sentenced to ten years' imprisonment. The court then turned to the girl, Florence:

the Inspector said in the interests of the girl she ought to be sent away (Hear, hear). Supt Pearson said he would communicate with Miss Wright, and see if she would admit the girl into the Rescue Home at Chester. The girl consented to go to the Home, but, crying bitterly, asked how long she would have to stay? The Mayor: 'As soon as you have learned to be a good girl'.

As soon as Tomlinson was again released on a conditional licence he was convicted of assault and gross indecency in 1918. He was sentenced to two months in prison. There can be little doubt that by now Tomlinson was a serial and serious sex offender who preyed upon young children. We would expect there to be a continued record of offending stretching into the early to mid-twentieth century. Fortunately for his potential victims, and maybe even for himself, Joseph alias James Tomlinson died aged 60 in 1920.

17. Lottie Gallon (b.1867) and Elizabeth Arnold (b.1848)

There are many more studies of male criminals than females, more boys than girls. Criminologists assert that women commit fewer crimes, and there is evidence from all countries and in all periods that there are far fewer females prosecuted in the courts than males. So we are always dealing with a smaller set of women to look at.

There is also the problem of tracing those women in the records. If they married, they often changed their surnames; if they moved in with a man they often took his surname even if they were not married in the traditional sense. Men often spoke for women when the census date came around, telling the census officer how old their wives were and what occupation they had, and they did not always get this information right, so that makes the women even harder to trace. Even when we have good quality criminal records to study, ensuring that we have the right woman is still tricky, as the cases of Lottie Gallon and Eliza Arnold illustrate.

Lottie was born in Staffordshire in 1867. On 10 May 1886 she was convicted of stealing a watch at Liverpool and sentenced to three months' imprisonment. Either side of this offence she gave birth to two daughters, Mary in 1885 and her namesake Lottie in 1887. By 1891 she was married and had changed her surname to Callaghan. She was a domestic housekeeper and her husband was absent on census night, so we do not know much about him (had they split up by then? Was he away working? We don't know). Five years later Lottie was sentenced to prison for stealing money (in January 1896) and for stealing clothes in November 1896. It is beginning to look as though her husband (if they had, indeed, been married) was no longer supporting the family. On 14 May 1897 she was given a two-week prison sentence for theft, and on the day she was released she was arrested for another theft. This time she served twenty-one days. She received another month in prison on 28 June 1897 for stealing some clothes. If it was the lack of a male 'breadwinner' to bring in a wage-packet that was causing her to steal, then her marriage to bricklayer Richard Child may have ended her offending.

Unfortunately, the pattern of committing low-value thefts and being locked up in prison for a few weeks at a time was too firmly established. Laundrywoman Lottie Child was convicted of stealing sheets on 29 May 1898; of helping a child to escape from Lichfield reformatory (this may have been either Mary or Lottie Gallon, both of whom were often before the courts); and of stealing blankets from Seacombe Laundry, Birkenhead, in 1899.

In 1900 she served six months for another theft, but was only back home living with her family for a short time before serving another six months' in custody. Released from Stafford prison on 13 April 1903, she said that she was heading for an address in Lichfield rather than Birkenhead. Perhaps she intended to see her daughter Lottie (who was possibly the child she was trying to liberate from Lichfield Reformatory School for Girls). However, although we can trace Lottie junior in 1911 as resident in another institution, we cannot find any further information on her mother. She does not appear in the 1911 census. Had she died by then? Had she remarried and taken another man's surname? Did she get left out of the census for some reason, or have we just 'missed her' in our endeavours to find her?

* * *

Lottie Gallon (Callaghan, Child) was hard to trace, and so was London-born Eliza Arnold. The 1851 census records Eliza as being born in Wapping in 1848, and now living in Limehouse workhouse in East London's docklands. The Stepney Poor Law Union was housing her as a 'pauper scholar'. An Elizabeth Arnold then appears on the criminal registers in 1859. This would make her 11 years old, if it is the same person. The fact that the registers say she already had two previous convictions and that she was sentenced to three years' penal servitude makes it unlikely that these two entries were, in fact, talking about the same person. Was the woman sentenced to three years perhaps 'our' Elizabeth's mother?

In 1861 the census records Elizabeth Arnold, aged 13, as an inmate and scholar at the Mile End Old Town Industrial School (part of the workhouse). Again, an Elizabeth Arnold appears in the criminal registers a year later. Again, she received a three-year 'stretch' for breaking into a dwelling house. Elizabeth's mother again, perhaps? This would at least explain why our Elizabeth was being looked after in the workhouse or the industrial school (where she would have been regarded as being at risk of delinquency).

In 1867 we can be fairly sure that we have rediscovered our Elizabeth. She was prosecuted at the Old Bailey alongside her friend Elizabeth Giddens. The two girls were charged with burglary of the Reverend Peter McCarthy's house, and having stolen property in their possession. The trial notes (which can be found in the Old Bailey Online website: www.oldbaileyonline.org), stated:

> [the householder's evidence] I went downstairs and found the whole of the lower part of the house ransacked, and the window in the back door broken, so that a person from the outside could undo the bolts ... then the door was easily opened, and an entrance effected into the front kitchen, and the property, plate, linen, boots and shoes, and fifteen or sixteen coats were all taken away ... I had heard considerable noise during the night, but

there was a hurricane blowing that evening, quite a gale, and my house is large and old – there was a good deal of rattling of windows and doors, and I conceived that all the noise was caused by the wind ...

[the witness's statement] I am a cabdriver in Leather Lane – on the morning of 8th January, about five o'clock or five minutes past, I was on the cab-stand near the Eagle Tavern, City Road – the two prisoners came up to me, Arnold first; she asked if I would go up to River Terrace, and take up – at that time Gibbons was standing a little distance off, on the pavement – they both got into the cab – they pulled me up at the corner of Alfred Street – I have since seen the prosecutor's house; it was a few yards from there ... when Gibbons met Arnold on the pavement with a bundle; they put it into the cab and got in, and I drove off ... she then got out of the cab, and went into a house – at that time the police constable came up, and took them into custody – I did not see any men with the prisoners.

[the police officer's evidence] I saw Arnold get out of the cab, and Gibbons was in the act of getting out; I told her to stop there, and asked what she had got there; she said they were Arnold's things, that she had left her place that morning – Arnold had then gone into the house – this is the bundle [*producing it*] ... it was tied up in this cloth, and contained five sheets, five pairs of boots, two dresses, two night dresses, two sheets, and several other articles – I asked her where she got these things – she made no answer – I then told them both to get into the cab, and directed the cabman to drive to the station.

[Gibbons' defence] All I have got to say is, the men came and asked me to carry the things, and I did. They said they would make me a handsome present, and, being an unfortunate girl, not knowing where to get a breakfast, I went for the sake of the money to get myself a breakfast in the morning. They gave me half a crown to get a cab. Arnold called for the cab.

[Arnold's defence] I left my home to go to work in the afternoon; instead of going to work, I went to Gibbons' house to have some tea. We went out and went to the play. It was too late for me to return home, and she said I could come home with her. I stayed with her all night. At four in the morning she woke me up; there were three men in the room; they asked her would she go and carry a bundle. She went, and I did the same as any other girl would do, because I would not stay there by myself.

The court found both girls guilty and Gibbons was imprisoned for eighteen months but Arnold, crucially, already had a previous conviction and was therefore sentenced to seven years' penal servitude. Sentences of imprisonment were served inside a local prison, but longer penal servitude sentences were served in a convict prison.

Elizabeth was a combative convict. She was punished with a bread and water diet in 1868 for 'kicking her cell door', and admonished for fighting with another female convict. More bread and water followed in 1869 for 'being disorderly', and she was kept in solitary confinement for further acts of disobedience in the next two years (fighting, spitting at other prisoners, quarrelling, being disobedient, being disorderly and so on).

Elizabeth was released on conditional licence on 4 July 1871. Had she been released before April (the census date), we might have found where she went to live. She gave no forwarding address when she left the prison. There is a newspaper article that may refer to her: 'Eliza Arnold, aged 23, a domestic servant of 27 Wynton Road, Bermondsey, was admitted to Guy's Hospital, suffering from a fractured shoulder blade and severe scalp wounds, occasioned by a fall downstairs' (*The Times*, 27 April 1879). Was this her? The 1881 census has an unmarried 32-year-old (which would have been near enough Elizabeth's age) woman, working as a domestic servant in Mile End Old Town (the place where our Elizabeth was a workhouse inmate). Was this her?

The name Elizabeth Arnold crops up again in the next few years in the criminal registers for larceny and receiving stolen property in 1889, for which she received eighteen months in custody; in the census, still unmarried, in 1891 in Mile End; and again as an unmarried servant in 1901 (this time in Romford, East London). The last time we might catch a glimpse of our Elizabeth is in 1911, when she was an inmate in Lambeth Workhouse, aged 65. This is the right name and about the right age for the person we have been tracking, but was it her? No matter how hard we strive to discover all of the details of their lives, both Lottie and Elizabeth have kept some secrets from us.

18. Stephen Swain (1870–1933)

Stephen was born in Crewe into a fairly large family. His family could easily have dragged Stephen into a life of crime but, as we will see, it was the troubles of his own children that seemed to precipitate his decline into criminality.

In 1873 Stephen's 12-year-old brother Charles was prosecuted for shoplifting sweetmeats (offal) from a shop. However, being let off with a caution may have set Charles on a better course in life, and he gained an apprenticeship at Crewe railway works in 1875 when the local employer was experiencing a boom in orders (the year after Charles joined them they produced their 2000th railway engine). His brother Joseph did the same in 1881, both earning wages of four shillings a week.

In 1882 Stephen had his first brush with the law, being birched by PC Wynne for committing theft. Like his brothers, he then started as an apprentice at Crewe works, aged 14. The railway company employed 60 per cent of all the men in Crewe and fostered the growth of the industrial town. By 1887 the Swain brothers worked together at the works with 27,000 other men (and a small number of women), having seemingly put their earlier indiscretions behind them. By 1887 the works took up 116 acres, with over 37 acres of roofed workshops. Charles was 'laid off' from work in 1887 as a downturn hit the business (his character was assessed as 'good' and his ability 'fair'), but his brothers James and Samuel started work there in 1888 and 1891 respectively to keep the Swain family income steady.

In 1890 Stephen married Martha Shaw at Nantwich, and their first son Joseph was born in 1891. Things appeared to be going well. Brother Charles was prosecuted for drunkenness, but it was common for young men to be picked up for drinking to excess in this period. Then came the news that Stephen had 'received his cards' (was made redundant). His character and ability were both assessed as 'moderate', but his services were no longer needed. In the period from the 1860s to 1880 skilled labour was in short supply, and the works had full order books. By the 1890s the needed labour was unskilled and plentiful. Samuel's other brother James was dismissed from the works too, after nearly three years' good service. Stephen's father was brought to court a couple of times for drunkenness, and his brother William was prosecuted for a felony that was not proved in court.

Stephen and Martha had two more children, Ada in 1893 and Stephen in 1895, both born at Martha's mother's house in Northwich. Stephen's family continued to get into minor scrapes. His father was convicted of fighting in the street in 1896 and being drunk and disorderly in 1897, while his brother was prosecuted for having a chimney fire (not keeping your chimney swept and causing a fire was considered a public danger). His other brother William took a neighbour to court for assaulting him.

Samuel lost his job in 1897. Like his other brothers, he was laid off when he was out of his apprenticeship. Employers preferred to take on more apprentices at lower wages than employ men on adult wages. Times were getting harder for the Swain family. In 1897 Stephen was prosecuted for neglecting his family. The court ordered him to pay 'maintenance' deducted from his wages for the upkeep of the children. Samuel was prosecuted for larceny (theft of some chickens), and Stephen was prosecuted for being drunk and disorderly. Stephen was then prosecuted for an aggravated assault on his wife. The case was dismissed when neither he nor Martha turned up to court, but it was an indication that things were beginning to go badly wrong in Stephen's life, and with his wider family. His brother Samuel was convicted of vagrancy and his other brother William took Ellen Owen to court for stealing his purse and money. Ellen was a notorious figure around Crewe, known for her drunken behaviour and her habit of taking what was not hers. Both William and Samuel seemed to be living a dissolute life, and William was living in Nantwich workhouse by 1901.

Stephen seemed to be keeping his head above water, still living with the family in a rented property in a working-class area of Crewe. His sons, however, were beginning to get into trouble. In 1902 his namesake Stephen was convicted of taking a pork pie from a shop, and then was prosecuted again (with Joseph Swain) for the theft of cocoa and toffees. Then both boys were again prosecuted for stealing cigarettes, and again for throwing stones (being 'a nuisance'). This was all within a twelve-month period. The following year young Stephen Swain, now aged 8, was convicted of stealing some pigeons. The court hearing was adjourned originally as the boy had run away from home. The local newspapers reported that Swain jnr 'had been up two or three times before for stealing, but under the misrepresentation of his father and mother, that the boy was under the age of 7, and they were unable to take proceedings against him. Superintendent Pearson obtained defendant's birth certificate and found the boy was over 8 years old'. This was an important legal distinction which meant that the court officials could now take the kind of action they were obviously longing for (see Chapter Three). Having established his age, the police and the courts punished the boy by sending him to Macclesfield Industrial School until he was 16; they punished his father by prosecuting him for 'conducing a youthful offender by neglect'. Stephen snr got drunk – and was arrested yet again. By this time his young daughter was also coming before the courts. Ada Swain had repaid the aunt who had taken her in, because her own family was not capable of looking after her, by stealing some of her money.

In 1905 14-year-old Joseph Swain was sent to the *Akbar* training ship for two years for stealing rabbits from a Crewe warehouse. He was also convicted of street gambling, obstructing the highway (selling bananas from a cart) and using obscene language (perhaps when the police stopped him selling his bananas). Steven snr was found to be drunk in the Red Bull Inn, and refusing to leave. That wasn't the reason he was gaoled though: he was still incapable or unwilling to pay the parental contribution for keeping his children in the various industrial schools. The *Crewe Chronicle* reported that his wife was 'a hardworking woman. They had four children, and she was trying to keep them by going out to work.' They had no food or fire in the house, and Stephen snr was now in prison for seven days.

In 1906 Joseph picked up his tenth conviction, followed quickly by a few others for again obstructing the highway (selling fish as well as bananas this time), playing street football and throwing stones at Crewe's Isolation Hospital. His father was back in prison in 1906 and 1907 for getting into arrears with his industrial school contributions.

Perhaps the strains in the Swain household were building. In 1907 Stephen snr was due to appear in court for committing an aggravated assault (what today would be called Actual Bodily Harm, Section 47 of the 1861 Offences Against the Person Act) on his wife Martha. Martha did not appear to give evidence (as was quite common in this period, and which, unfortunately, is still the case today), and the case was dismissed.

Over the next few years both Stephen and his sons were convicted of many offences, including playing street football, theft of poultry and drunkenness, and the newspaper reports were frank: 'The Prisoner would not work, he was seen that morning with a bottle of beer for breakfast. He was a worthless fellow.' More offending followed in the run-up to the First World War.

In 1914 Stephen was again due to appear in court to answer yet another summons after having ignored two previous court summons. The police executed a warrant granted by the magistrates to drag him from his house. The Superintendent explained that 'Swain's wife lay dead in the house and he did not wish to press the case' – the case was dismissed (*Crewe Chronicle*, 15 August 1914). Stephen himself died in 1933.

Stephen was born into a family where offending was commonplace, and had had an early brush with the law himself. He could quite easily have fallen into a lifetime of offending like his brothers, but he found a job and a wife and initially kept out of the courts. However, the environment that he could not escape caught up with him in the end. The casual employment and dismissal of employees from Crewe Works (especially when they became expensive), the inability to keep control and to pay for his children, the tensions in the house, and (presumably) the temptations of a drink with his brothers when things got too much meant that, having escaped the lure of offending as a youth, Stephen tumbled back into it when he was middle-aged.

19. William Brisbane (1882–1976)

William Brisbane seems to have lived a normal and unremarkable life until his early teens, living with his parents and siblings in Newton, Manchester, until 1894. Sadly for William, his mother Mary then died, leaving his grief-stricken father with three children to cope with. It appears that he struggled, for William was convicted at Hyde magistrates court for being 'found wandering and not having proper guardianship' in June 1895. This was not his first time in court, however. William had several previous convictions for thefts committed since his mother died. The courts ordered that William should be admitted to Stockport industrial school to be kept there until he was 16 years old.

This duly took place, and William was released in 1898. His notes state that his 'Father is Robert Brisbane, 7 George Street, Victoria Street, Newton, Factory Operative. Indifferent character. Mother dead', so William was released into the care of his uncle, George Brisbane. Uncle George, a hat-maker, had offered both to look after the boy and also to help him to find employment, which he did, in a nearby cotton mill.

By 1900, however, William had gone to live with his father at Bolton. A year later he was renting a room in a lodging house and working as a labourer in an ironworks. He did not settle there either, and his School Board report (for Stockport continued to keep a watchful eye over William) stated that he was working as a travelling crane-operator for the London & North Western Railway Company. He was, however, still resident in Bolton, which suggests that he had some stability in his life, and the school inspector reported that he was pleased with William's progress. He was recorded as having a 'good character'. He had not committed any further offences, and at the age of 21 he seemed to be settling down. There were further indications of this in 1907, when he married a young woman from Bolton, Alice Bennett. Their daughter Edith was born in the city the following year.

The 1911 census records that William lived in a four-bedroom house at 40 Darbishire Street, Bolton, with his family, and still worked at the iron foundry. In 1915 another child joined the family, and William, although in an occupation that exempted him from joining up, enlisted in the army. He was considered fit for home service: '5 feet 6½ [inches tall], with a girth of 35½ inches when fully expanded. His vision and physical development is good.' He then spent a couple of years in three regiments, fighting in the trenches, and making it through to the last stages of the First World War without serious injury. But on 18 July 1917 he was gassed. Mustard gas was the most well-known form of chemical warfare used in the First World War. It was, however, only used in the last two years of the war (although other gaseous toxins had been used since 1915). Mustard gas did not kill all of the soldiers who were exposed to it. However, those men who did not die from its immediate toxic impact suffered considerable long-term damage to their skin, eyes and lungs, as William did.

Soldiers feared and dreaded the prospect of being gassed. Mustard gas drifted across the trenches like a deadly fog, causing panic with every change in wind speed and direction. Home-made gas-masks (usually socks doused with urine and wrapped around the face) had been replaced with rudimentary gas-masks by 1917, but they were unreliable and difficult to use. The war poet Wilfred Owen accurately conveyed the sense of panic, powerlessness and horror that mustard gas engendered whenever it was used:

Gas! GAS! Quick, boys! – An ecstasy of fumbling, Fitting the clumsy helmets just in time; But someone still was yelling out and stumbling, And flound'ring like a man in fire or lime ... Dim, through the misty panes and thick green light, As under a green sea, I saw him drowning. In all my dreams, before my helpless sight, He plunges at me, guttering, choking, drowning.

These lines from *Dulce et Decorum Est* (1917) echo the words of writer, pacifist and wartime nurse Vera Brittain. In her chronicle of the war, *Testament of Youth* (1933), she wrote:

I wish those people who talk about going on with this war whatever it costs could see the soldiers suffering from mustard gas poisoning. Great mustard-coloured blisters, blind eyes, all sticky and stuck together, always fighting for breath, with voices a mere whisper, saying that their throats are closing and they know they will choke.

In November 1917 the British Army captured a stockpile of German-made mustard gas shells at Cambrai. The British then worked to develop their own version of the gas, and deployed it in September 1918. Had the war not ended soon afterwards, the British use of mustard gas might well have increased, since the war-strategists considered it to be an effective weapon.

William was demobbed (discharged) from the army on 22 February 1919 and awarded a disability pension. We do not know much more about William's life until he died, aged 78, in Farnworth, Bolton, in 1960. William had been various things in life: thief, neglected-child, industrial school inmate, husband, father, worker, soldier, war-hero, possibly a grandfather, and long-term resident of Bolton. He coped with many difficulties as a child, but he fought to overcome his problems and both as a young man and as an adult he managed to make a good life for himself and his family.

20. Thomas Henry Platt (b.1884)

Thomas was born in Lymm, Cheshire, in 1884. His mother, Mary Ann Platt, was an unmarried woman from Liverpool. She was frequently prosecuted for soliciting (prostitution), drunkenness and using obscene language. The identity of Thomas's father is not known, nor that of the father of his younger brother Samuel. The boys were said to be neglected by their mother, who could not or would not take care of them.

Samuel, born in 1887, was too young to be sent to an industrial school, so he was placed in Dutton Workhouse near Daresbury, Cheshire. In the early to mid-nineteenth century children made up nearly half of all workhouse inmates, sometimes staying there with their parents, sometimes on their own. One-third of the 200 inmates of the Nantwich Union Workhouse in 1881 were babies and children aged 16 or under, most of them housed in a workhouse school on the same site. One-fifth of Stockport Union Workhouse's 520 inmates were children aged up to 16, and more were housed in its network of six 'scattered homes' (www.workhouse.org.uk and www.childrens homes.org.uk). All of the children in the workhouse received a basic education, and were sometimes made to work for local employers during their time in the workhouse. Samuel went to work for a barge-man on the canals in Manchester, and boarded at his master's house until he was in his twenties.

Thomas was old enough to be placed in an industrial school, but at the age of 6 he was charged with not being under proper guardian-ship at Altrincham magistrates court on 19 October 1890. He was sent to Stockport Industrial School until he was 14 (when he could go out and find work for himself). Eight years was a long time for him to be placed 'in care' and he was fairly young to be institutionalised in this way, but his case was not unusual. There were many very young children living in industrial and reformatory schools in this period.

Stockport Industrial School was originally built as a vicarage and served as a school dedicated to the education of destitute children (such enterprises were sometimes known as 'ragged schools') before being certified by the Home Office as an industrial school in 1866. The school managed to raise sufficient funds from local charities and benefactors to extend its premises in the 1860s. It could now hold 150 inmates, which included boys and girls until the girls were removed to the new Stockport Industrial School for Girls in 1877. The school accepted children from a wide geographical area, with a large con-tingent from Belper in Derbyshire. Belper was a strong Methodist town and the school was criticised for appearing to favour the Methodists over other religions. Nevertheless, the school was recog-nised by government inspectors as an exemplary institution, especi-ally renowned for its cost-effectiveness. The school moved to new premises in 1898 when the original site was beyond reasonable repair, and it became an Approved School in 1933.

The boys in its care were subject to a strict regime. They rose from their beds at 5.30am, swept and cleaned their dormitories, washed themselves, attended physical drill (exercises and marching) and were then inspected before they were allowed to have breakfast at

8.30am. They were required to attend band practice every day, and a religious service on Tuesdays. They could look forward to a hot bath on Thursdays and Fridays, and bedtime every night at 8.30pm. Sunday involved a trip to Sunday school for religious instruction, as well as two church services and prayers during breakfast. They did, however, get a lie-in on Sundays, till 7.30am. They also received hot meals. The fare was 'solid' but nutritious, mainly consisting of bread and porridge for breakfast, and lots of lentils, cabbage, bread and tinned meat for main meals (pudding was cocoa and more bread, but sweetened with syrup).

The boys were typically trained in the textile trades (Stockport was a centre of hat-making and the silk industry). The idea was that they would pick up practical skills which would enable them to find work when they left, and also learn punctuality, self-discipline, politeness and a good attitude to life and work for the future.

On 3 December 1897 Thomas was released from this regime on conditional licence. The school had found him work as an errand boy in a nearby iron merchant's warehouse. He lodged first with a local landlady, Mrs Fallows, at 40 Worrall Street in Stockport, then with two other landladies, still in Stockport. His employer, Mr Parkes, seemed to be pleased with his progress. The school recorded that he was doing 'fairly well' in December 1899, but he desired a change of occupation and started to work for his landlady's husband in 1900. Now a greengrocer's assistant, he was again said by the school authorities to be 'doing well'. That was in 1900. A year later he had changed his occupation again, becoming a farm labourer at Lostock Hall, Poynton, Cheshire. It is not clear how long he stayed as a farm-hand, but he clearly still had itchy feet as in 1911 he was boarding at 38 Adswood Lane West in Stockport and working as a chauffeur.

Both Thomas and his younger brother Samuel survived to become employed young men. The official record stops at this point, and the census is not available past 1911, so it is difficult to follow either man beyond their twenties.

21. Elizabeth Barratt (b.1896), Alice Midgley (b.1902) and Henry Burrows (b.1881)

As seen in Chapter Three, the reformatories and industrial schools forced a system of care and control on to children who had either committed, or were in danger of committing, offences. The system tried to replicate parental discipline and affection within an institutional framework. The kinds of children it sought to guide and train were those who were beyond the control of their parents, or those whose parents neglected their duties. For example, Elizabeth, Alice and Henry were all taken into Stockport industrial schools in the early twentieth century.

Born on 19 October 1896, Elizabeth Barratt lived with her grandmother. Her mother died sometime between 1896 and 1901 (possibly giving birth to Elizabeth). When she was admitted to Stockport Industrial School for Girls in October 1907, her notes said:

> For years she and her brother had been sent out into the streets to sell firewood and she has been known to sleep out all night. Her mother is dead. The girl is illegitimate. Father been sent to prison for neglecting his children. An idle, careless, lazy man. He is a labourer who spends most of his time at a lodging house kept by his mother at 1 Oldfield Court, Mowbray Street, Middle Hillgate, Stockport.

This address was different from the grandparents', but wherever she had been living Elizabeth was, in the eyes of the authorities, 'not under proper guardianship'. She had not committed any offences, but she was clearly a vulnerable child. The State stepped in, and she was sent to the industrial school until she reached the age of 16. As a young female inmate, she would have been trained in sewing, laundry and learning domestic service. Just as industrial school boys were a ready supply of labour for factories and the armed forces, so girls were channelled from the schools directly into domestic service at the age of 16. The schools were therefore trying to provide employment that society considered suitable for the children of working-class parents, and also to replace the care and affection that could never be provided by parents who had died or been imprisoned, or who had simply walked away from their responsibilities.

* * *

Alice Midgley was born in 1902 in Altrincham, near Manchester. She lived with her three siblings and her parents, who, in 1911, were about to celebrate their tenth wedding anniversary. However, sometime before 1916 Alice's mother was confined in a county asylum (reason unknown). In 1916 Alice was convicted of burglary at Altrincham Juvenile Court, and at the age of 13 she was required by the courts to stay in Stockport Industrial School for Girls for three years. Her case file stated:

> Her father is John Midgley, milling machinist, who lives at 32 Ashton Avenue, Altrincham. Character and circumstances are good. Respectable, good, working-class home. Her mother is in the asylum. Her Aunt keeps house. Previous character: Bad. Stealing money from home. She has given a great deal of trouble. Frequently run away from home. Often travelled long distances by train and been successful in eluding the railway company.

Official reports do not say whether Alice's bad behaviour started when her mother was placed in an asylum, but life must have been difficult for a teenage girl being brought up by a single parent. Of course, many parents left their children for their own reasons, not through death or imprisonment.

*   *   *

Henry Burrows' parents got married, aged 19, when Henry's mother was already pregnant. Eight years later Henry was convicted of truancy and not being under proper guardianship and was sent to Stockport Industrial School for eight years (when he would be 16 years old). His case file noted that his mother was a charwoman and his father was dead. His mother was required to pay three shillings a week as a contribution towards Henry's upkeep while he was in the school. This would have been a considerable burden for a single parent surviving on a charwoman's meagre wages. But was Henry's father really dead? In the 1891 census Henry's mother was listed as 'married' not as 'widowed', and the death of a John Burrows in Stockport aged 39 was registered in 1897. Was this Henry's father? Only after 1897 did Henry's mother record her status as 'widowed'. In any case Henry seems to have got on with his life after he was released from the school.

Henry returned to his mother's house in 1897 and took a job as an errand boy. A year later he was a barman, and the school authorities recorded that he was 'doing well'. In 1906, aged 25, Henry married Mary in Stockport; five years later they were still living in Stockport, but now in a five-bedroomed house in a nice part of town. Henry ran a flourishing greengrocery and Mary was his assistant. Henry died in 1949, aged 67, and his wife died in 1951.

Henry and Alice (who married in 1948 and died aged 61 in 1962) both seem to have survived the disruption in the early part of their lives. In Henry's case the absence of a father did not prevent him making a great success of his life. The industrial schools, like the reformatories, when they worked as they were intended to provided a family-type environment which stabilised many of the children who were grieving for lost parents, or were escaping negligent and violent parents (see Chapters Two and Three).

22. John O'Sullivan (1896–1916)

John's parents married in June 1896, the same month that John was born. The family lived in Maynard Street in Liverpool, with John's father working as a labourer at a local iron foundry. John could reasonably have expected to follow in his father's footsteps or to pick up another kind of industrial job in his home town. However, he got into trouble when he was in his early teens, and the magistrates sent him to the *Akbar* training ship on 12 April 1910.

The *Akbar* was moored in the River Mersey with other training ships, including the *Conway*, the *Clarence* (which was for Catholic boys) and the *Indefatigable* (for orphaned children). The *Akbar* was reserved for Protestant boys. All of the training ships in Liverpool were set up by charities and benefactors and were later licensed by the Home Office as certified juvenile reformatories. The Liverpool Juvenile Reformatory Association also ran the Mount Vernon Reformatory for Girls and the Liverpool Farm School in Newton-le-Willows.

Training ships on the River Mersey (http://www.liverpoolpicturebook.com/2013/08/merseyside-training-ships.html).

INDEFATIGABLE

Due to its poor physical state, the *Akbar* was scrapped in 1907. After being housed in a temporary camp for eighteen months, over 200 boys were rehoused in the new Akbar Nautical School for Boys at Heswall (onshore, further along the Mersey) in 1909. The new reformatory premises were ready and waiting for John when he was sent there for five years in 1910. However, there were deep problems in the reformatory. The *Akbar* had long attracted an unwelcome reputation. The ship was synonymous with scandal. In 1887 boys set fire to the ship in one of the most dramatic of many mutinies to break out on these hulks. In October 1910 the *John Bull* newspaper broke news of a series of alleged serious abuses, which prompted the then Home Secretary, Winston Churchill, to establish the Departmental Committee on Reformatory and Industrial Schools. The committee later published a highly critical report in 1913 prompting a wider reform of the whole system, but the scandals continued. In the 1940s the superintendent resigned following more allegations, this time about indecency. The school was finally closed in 1956.

Back in 1910 John received an elementary education, mainly reading and writing classes. His progress was poor; the Heswall Progress Register reported that he was 'very backward', although he 'seemed to be a cheerful boy'. Two years later the records show he was 'More or less characterless ... easily led astray ... Unmanly, but keeps steady when under strict discipline ... Has improved generally but unfortunately is neither trustworthy nor truthful ... unreliable and of weak character. Does moderately well under discipline and supervision. Cheerful temperament.'

Although John did not seem to be very bright academically, the reformatory staff did envisage a possible career for him. Training ships were part of a tradition that went back to the eighteenth-century Marine Societies that trained boys for life in the merchant navy on release. The training regime involved hard physical tasks such as swabbing the decks, tailoring, shoemaking and oakum-picking (distending old navy rope), although this practice had been abandoned by the time John boarded the ship. Nevertheless, John received sufficient training to get him a job at sea.

The reformatory operated a licensing system (similar to the one that operated in Van Diemen's Land, see Chapter Three) and managed to procure John a place in the merchant navy in April 1913. Unfortunately, things did not work out. The reports state that John was 'not quite normal minded ... very slovenly and uncouth'.

He was readmitted to Heswall in September 1914. The reformatory staff were now presented with another option for John.

In the autumn of 1914, with war declared, men flocked to sign up to join the armed forces. Liverpool men answered Lord Derby's plea to fight for King and Country. Thousands of volunteers turned up to the King's Regiment headquarters in St Anne Street on 28 August 1914. Lord Derby had declared, 'This should be a Battalion of Pals, a battalion in which friends from the same office will fight shoulder to shoulder for the honour of Britain and the credit of Liverpool.' There were not enough volunteers to form one regiment; there were enough for three. By November there were four Liverpool 'Pals' regiments.

John was licensed to the 1st City Battalion, Kings Liverpool Regiment on 1 November 1914. Bugler O'Sullivan, regimental number 17/21996, received army pay of one shilling a day, and free food. Like many boys on the *Akbar*, and in other similar institutions, John had learned how to play a musical instrument while he was in the reformatory. As a bugler, his job would have been to march in front of the soldiers who were going 'over the top' in trench warfare – a truly terrifying prospect, especially for someone so young.

After their training was completed, it was announced that the Pals would be leaving for France on 31 October 1915. In March 1916 Liverpool newspapers reported some sad news:

'KILLED IN ACTION' – Mrs O'Sullivan, of 15 Linden Street, Liverpool, has received news that her son, Drummer O'Sullivan, of the 17th Service Battalion The King's (Liverpool Regiment) (1st 'Pals') has been killed in action, his death being instantaneous. He joined the 'Pals' at the outbreak of the war and was drafted to France in November. He was 19 years of age and previously a scholar of the Chatsworth Street School. His lieutenant speaks very highly of his bravery and his great popularity with his comrades.

The Heswall School Report of 19 March 1916 noted that they had received additional news from the front. John had apparently been shot in the trenches by a sniper while he was reading a letter sent from home; he died instantaneously. Many of his comrades were killed in the Battle of the Somme later in 1916, while others died in subsequent battles during the conflict. Indeed, of the four original Liverpool Pals battalions that sailed to France in November 1915,

20 per cent did not survive to see the end of the war. Although this figure is itself alarming, if we add together all of those who were wounded, and those who were transferred from the Pals to other regiments (and subsequently killed), the casualty figure rises to nearly 75 per cent.

John might never have signed up to take the King's shilling in 1914 if he had not been placed in a reformatory. Perhaps none of the reformatory boys who joined up, and died in the trenches, would have joined up. However, given that thousands of young Liverpudlians just like John were happy to 'do their bit', it is entirely possible that he would have done so anyway. There is no reason to think that reformatory boys were any less patriotic than other young men, and like other young men in the First World War, they died in their thousands (see Chapter Two).

23. George Edwards (1904–1927)

George already had three brothers and two sisters when he was born on 3 January 1904. Four more brothers would follow before he was 6 years old. In 1911 the whole family lived at 56 Clarendon Street, Birkenhead, with George's father working as a labourer for the local authority and his wife of seventeen years looking after the children at home. It was only a couple of years later that George first started to get into trouble. He was prosecuted for stealing two shillings and a pawn ticket. The pawnbroker was a vital support for working-class communities in this period. When the weekly wage could not be eked out, people pawned a suit, a watch or some other property in return for a 'loan'. When they handed in their ticket and a fee to the pawnbroker, they had their property returned. So, in stealing a ticket, George was really depriving someone of a valuable piece of property. For these offences he received a probation order.

There had been various experiments by religious bodies, and sympathetic policy-makers, in providing assistance to defendants who needed guidance in the courtroom, and support following their sentences. In 1876 the Church of England Temperance Society funded two men who attended police courts in Southwark looking for people who had problems with alcohol (and who were reformable). They were very much seen as domestic 'missionaries' who journeyed into the heart of the city to rescue the morally weak, in the same way that their colleagues were converting 'natives' to Christianity in Africa. The system of 'police court missionaries' spread across London. By

1880 there were eight full-time missionaries in place, organised by the London Police Courts Mission. In 1886 the Probation of First Time Offenders Act allowed courts around the country to establish their own system. Few did so. However, in 1907 the Probation of Offenders Act bestowed official status on the missionaries (and in 1908 they became known as probation officers). The Act allowed courts to discharge defendants if they pledged to keep out of trouble for between one and three years. During that time they would be 'supervised' by their probation officer. As youths were thought to be more easily reformed than adults (see Chapter Two), the 1927 Molony Committee encouraged the informal involvement of probation officers in supervising borstal and reformatory school children after they left their institutions.

George was still in his first year on probation and under supervision when he stole a purse in November 1914. For this, he was birched at the police station. The six strokes were usually administered by the biggest police officer in the station, so as to provide as intimidating an experience as possible. But that didn't work with George either. A few months after his birching he was found in Birkenhead Market Hall 'for unlawful purposes'. The magistrates turned to the Albert Memorial Industrial School in Birkenhead to help reform George. In 1915 he was sent there, to remain until he was 16 years old. Conditions within these institutions are described in Chapter Three, and the overcrowded and gloomy (according to an 1896 Report) Albert Memorial Industrial School is described in more detail on Peter Higginbotham's Children's Homes website (http://www.childrenshomes.org.uk/BirkenheadAlbert/).

The industrial school system also seems to have had little impact on George. Almost as soon as he was released, he was convicted of theft at Birkenhead, and the magistrates turned to another form of supervision. Bradwall Reformatory would next have the pleasure of George's company, this time for four years, until he was 19 years old.

Bradwall Reformatory kept annual reports on all of its inmates. In July 1919 it reported that George was a 'rather rough type, good at farm work, particularly with horses'. They seemed quite pleased with him, and he was licensed to leave (with conditions to keep him on the straight and narrow) on 2 October 1922. The same day he joined the East Lancashire Regiment at their Preston recruitment office. He lasted three months before being discharged from the regiment for having 'physical problems' and 'defects'. He was then out of work, and remained so for a few months before he returned to Brad-wall Reformatory to ask for help. It found him employment with Mr Garnett, of Manor Farm, Middlewich. A month later he left Mr Garnett to work for Mr Kennerley, a farmer in Holmes Chapel. Both Middlewich and Holmes Chapel are only a few miles away from Bradwall Reformatory. Four months later he left Mr Kennerley's farm too. He didn't return to Bradwall and he didn't return to his parents. His father thought he might have emigrated to Canada (as many people were at that time). If he did cross the Atlantic, he was soon back again, asking for money for clothes at Bradwall. He then joined the Cheshire Regiment in 1924. Perhaps working on the farms had improved his physique and cured his defects and problems?

The Cheshire Regiment sent him for training at Strensall Military Camp in York, and the annual school report states that he was happy and doing very well. He was recommended as suitable for foreign service in 1925 (although he blotted his copybook by being late returning from leave, and riding his army-issue bicycle without lights, for which he served fourteen days' hard labour). The Birken-head Women Citizens Association – volunteers who raised funds, helped to secure employment, and monitored juvenile offenders – recorded that he was still in military service in 1926. By this time he was serving in India, and is again reported as 'doing well'. Unfor-tunately, just as George seemed to have found something he was happy doing, and was good at, he died in 1927 of acute mastoiditis. Today this complaint would be simply and quickly cured by a course of antibiotics.

The physical punishments that George experienced in his youth had little impact on him, and his first brush with supervision was also ineffective. Indeed, it was only the repeated help, supervision, guid-ance and practical support that Bradwall offered that made George suitable for employment and a crime-free life. Even then, it appears that the disciplined military environment kept George on the straight and narrow.

24. Walter Davenport (1906–1976)

Walter Davenport and his wife Ada lived at 21 Flint Street, Birken-head. Ada had given birth to eight children before Walter jnr was born in 1906, but three of the children had died. Infant mortality, particularly for boys, was consistently high, although things were improving. In the 1870s the infant mortality rate was approximately

15 per cent. By the 1930s it had halved to approximately 7 per cent. Nevertheless, working-class parents did not enjoy the health care, good nutrition levels and safe housing conditions of the middle and upper classes, so the mortality rate was always much higher in households like the one into which Walter jnr was born.

Aged 13, Walter already had two convictions for theft before he was convicted of a felony at Birkenhead Magistrates' Court. In 1908 they sent him to Bradwall Training School in the Cheshire country-side for five years, along with about seventy other boys who were housed in the well-regarded reformatory. Its originator and manager George Latham was a Crewe magistrate, a member of the Cheshire Chamber of Agriculture and, briefly in later life, the Liberal MP for Crewe. He dedicated thirty years to establishing a training and super-vision regime for children who were sent to Bradwall from the locality, and also from further afield (there was a large London con-tingent). Latham drew on his farming and other networks to raise support for the school, and to arrange apprenticeships for the Brad-wall children with local farmers; although Latham died in 1886, those networks were still in place when Walter was placed at the school in 1919.

When it was time for Walter to be released on conditional licence in 1923, the agricultural connections the reformatory had developed were not thought suitable for Walter, and he was found a position with steam-ship repairers Clover Clayton & Co. in his home town of Birkenhead. He moved back in with his parents, but only for a short period. His mother told the Bradwall that he had left home to live in London in November 1924. It transpired that Walter had been accused of stealing three pounds from his parents in order to finance his London adventure. When Walter was visited by the Bradwall Superintendent at his 'digs' in the New Kent Road, he stated that his father got drunk at the weekends and that they quarrelled constantly. The lodger in his parents' house advised him to move away, and indeed came down to London with him, with both of them working as bartenders. Walter must have gone back to Birkenhead at some point, however, as he was prosecuted at Chester Assizes on a charge of burglary and was sent back to reform school on 22 June 1925. A week later he absconded on a bicycle, and made it across the water to Liverpool, where he was apprehended the next day and returned to the school. Four days later he absconded again. But there were further problems to come for Walter. After his release, the Bradwall authorities received a letter from Walter who was on remand in Liverpool Prison. On 20 October 1925 he was sentenced at Birkenhead Sessions to three years' borstal training (see Chapter Three). He served his time at Her Majesty's Borstal Institution, Portland. The borstal at Portland had been established a few years earlier to receive boys from other borstals who were disruptive, as well as new entries like Walter. Fortunately, Walter had left before a German aircraft bombed Portland in 1940, leaving four boys dead and numerous others injured.

Again Walter did not manage to complete his licence period successfully. Returning to Cheshire, he committed thefts with another boy and, after serving fourteen days' hard labour, he was returned to Portland Borstal in January 1928. After this, finally free of penal institutions, Walter's life was on the up. He married in 1934. He was safely back in his home town of Birkenhead, and he seems to have settled down. He does not appear in any criminal records, and we next see him in an official record in 1978, when his death in Ellesmere Port, near Birkenhead, is recorded.

Walter Davenport died only forty years ago, so his children and grandchildren may be alive and may read this book. Thus, we have an ethical duty to treat the data we have on Walter with sensitivity and with respect (see Chapter Two). We decided not to give Walter a pseudonym because we think his story is an important one, and one that deserves to be told. He had a hard life, with many brushes with the law, but he came through it, got married and never reoffended. We don't know if Walter (and his descendants) would approve of the way we have 'connected the historical dots' to tell his story, but we do know that his story can provide important lessons for researchers of youth crime and punishment.

25. Jane Jones (b.1908)

Jane Jones was born in 1908. Twenty years later, in 1928, she married Peter Price, who was one year her senior. Later that same year she gave birth to a son, James. However, when James was just eight weeks old Jane was brought before the Manchester City Sessions charged with theft. Jane, who was 20 years of age by this point, was aided in her crimes by 18-year-old Anne Blair, who had been working as a shop assistant. Anne pleaded not guilty to stealing one dress from C&A Modes Ltd in Oldham Street, Manchester, and another dress from Lewis's Ltd, also in Manchester, in October 1928. Jane, on the other hand, pleaded guilty.

The *Evening Chronicle* asserted that Jane had a 'mania for dancing' and she frequented dance halls every night. The Recorder, Sir Walter Greaves Lord, ordered that the girls be sent to a borstal institution for three years so that they could be 'disciplined and trained'. The records officer also noted that Jane was married with a child, and consequently the recorder added that arrangements might be made for the child to be sent with her. 'Both girls broke down on hearing the decision, and had to be assisted from the court.' Jane was kept in Manchester Prison, also known as Strangeways, while waiting to be transferred to Aylesbury Borstal for Girls.

The recorder's suggestion that the child could be sent with Jane to a borstal caused great issues. In December 1928 the Governor of Aylesbury Borstal, L.C. Banks, stated:

> I should like to suggest that I think it would be the greatest mistake to send the baby here with the girl. We have several other cases of girls who have babies before they came here and I know that there would be great jealousy. Also it is always very difficult to discipline and train a girl who has to look after her baby as of necessity she cannot be free at all essential times. As the baby has now been separated from the mother for some time I should like to suggest that it is either kept at the hospital or union until the mother's discharge, if she has no relatives willing to take it. Personally I feel that it is rather a mistake to sentence a married woman to borstal detention. She will obviously be so much older in her ways than the majority of girls and this is always undesirable.

The governor, it seems, believed not only that the infant should not be sent to borstal but that neither should the mother, for very different reasons. It is true that Jane was at the upper age limit when she received her sentence. Nevertheless, the governor was informed that the commissioners had decided that the child should go to Aylesbury with the mother, as it was 'obviously the Recorder's wish'. He was further instructed to ascertain if Jane in fact wanted her child to go with her. Banks responded, 'This girl would be very glad to have her baby here, and we should be glad if it would be arranged.' He then raised no further objections but it was already June 1929. By this point James was around seven months old, having been born in December

1928, and had been separated from his mother for some time. There was another barrier to mother and baby being reunited: the child could not be sent to Aylesbury until he was free of infection. The Governor of Manchester Prison reported; 'Please note that the child should not be sent to Aylesbury' because of his infection and there are other infants in the institution:

> Dear Sir, re James Price H.S. No 164021.
> I am in receipt of your enquiry regarding the above-named, who's making very erratic progress. He is now taking his feeds much better, but his weight is still very up and down and he occasionally vomits. There is no present intention of discharging him.
> (Medical Superintendent)

It is impossible to imagine how Jane must have felt, knowing her child was ill but being unable to be with him. We do not know how many of the details were passed onto Jane about the health of her child but if she was made aware of the letters from the medical superintendent – for example, one stated that the 'child is not making satisfactory progress and his discharge is consequently indefinite'– it must have been distressing for her. The medical superintendent, Mr Gamble, informed the Governor of Strangeways that 'The child is suffering from Nasal Diphtheria' in June 1929. James was transferred from Manchester Union Booth Hall Infirmary, Blackley, Manchester to Withington Hospital, West Disbury. Finally, early in September 1929 James was removed into custody and isolated along with Jane. Mr Gamble, the medical officer, recommended that the infant should have a short period of quarantine before mixing with healthy children as 'a precautionary measure I should adopt were I in charge of the receiving institution'.

Aylesbury was the first borstal institution for girls. It was a converted reformatory for inebriates and in their critical survey *The Howard League for Penal Reform* stated that 'home-like is not an adjective that is applicable to it'. In their report, as late as 1945, the Prison Commissioners wrote 'the Commissioners have long regarded the position of Aylesbury as unsatisfactory'. They recommended more modern institutions for girls to be set up and classification to be implemented, and Aylesbury to be used only as an allocation centre. East Sutton Park, 'one brighter spot', was opened in 1946 as the first open institution for girls. This was too late for Jane. As is often the case within the justice system, females were thought of last or, as the Howard League put it, 'the girls have fared less well than the boys' in terms of buildings and occupations. The girls did have educational training but other than a few who worked in the gardens or on farms, most were employed in domestic work or chores throughout the time borstals were used. This problem seems to have arisen from both the lesser numbers of girls and there being little expected of them; as the Howard League remarked, their 'average intelligence is low' and 'they look forward to marriage as their natural end'. As a result, little choice of employment was laid before them. Indeed, L.W. Fox in his book *The English Prison and Borstal Systems* (1948) states that there are no options for these girls to learn vocational trades in borstal which they could follow upon release, but he adds a presumption that most of them would not have done so anyway, thus implying a lack of interest of the part of the girls.

Unfortunately, we do not know if Jane, upon release, went home to her husband. However, her story highlights the different issues which female offenders posed to the justice system, even within the borstal system. Jane was 'lucky' enough to be reunited with her son James, but many other female offenders in the same position were not. Even with a recommendation of the Recorder, and the insistence of the Police Commissioners, there was push-back from the institution itself.

26. Brendan Behan (1923–1964)

In his book *Borstal Boy* (1958) Brendan Behan wrote:

> It's great to be on your own for a bit. That's the thing you never were at Walton. Nor in any prison, I suppose. For all their solitary confinement you were watched and your every movement ...

Brendan Behan was from Dublin, and was 16 years of age when he made his way to Liverpool. He had only been there for forty-eight hours when he was arrested after being caught with explosives. In his own words: 'I came over to fight for the Irish workers and Small Farmers of the Republic, for a full and free life, for my countrymen, North and South, and for the removal of the baneful influence of British Imperialism from Irish affairs. God save Ireland.' Brendan was born in 1923 into a republican family; he became a member of the IRA's youth organisation by the age of 14, and joined the IRA by 16.

He was well educated in literature generally but particularly in Irish nationalist history and literature. He left school when he was 13 to become a painter, like his father. He had also passed the London City and Guilds examination in Painters Work, in the Day Apprentice School in Dublin. Upon arrest he was sent to Dale Street and put in a solitary cell where, on his first night, upon hearing the church bells in the distance, he said they 'made misery mark time'. In describing his first night in confinement he stated, 'a blunt and numbing pain it is, to wake up in a cell for the first time'. He was offered leniency by officials if he gave information on the IRA. But he either would not, or could not, and therefore said he knew nothing.

Brendan was only 16 years of age and so he should have been tried in the juvenile court but since that court did not have the authority to hear such a serious crime, he was sent to the magistrates' court instead. Meanwhile, he awaited his trial in Walton Prison. On arrival, he was told to turn out his pockets but he hid his cigarettes, a move which resulted in a beating. Shortly after this he was strip-searched and intimately examined. When he was finally taken to his cell he found he could 'walk five paces from the door to under the window', which he could not reach. He was kept separate from the adults along with the other young prisoners and overseen by specially trained officers. Brendan claimed to be treated especially harshly because he was an IRA man. He describes his time on remand as monotonous: scrubbing his cell every day and sewing mail bags. The highlight of his time there was that he was given two books a week, which he cherished. He was again beaten after he insulted a Roman Catholic priest, who had informed him that he would be excommunicated, as all IRA men were, unless he denounced his membership. This he refused to do.

In his autobiography Brendan describes how he dealt with bullies in Walton Prison. There were two other young prisoners, both older than him, who were bullying him. One he was afraid of but the other he decided to make an example of. He grabbed hold of him and hit him in the face until an officer (he called all officers 'screws') stopped him. This resulted in a bloody face for the boy, and solitary confinement, bread and water and no mattress for a day for Brendan. He had expected the punishment to be worse. He hoped this would result in others being afraid of him. During his time at the borstal he got into a couple of scuffles there too, but they were broken up by the officers and were not serious.

143

When Brendan finally made it to the Assizes, the trial was 'short and sweet' and as he put it, 'The stuff [explosives] had been caught with me and as a soldier of the Irish Republic Army I refused to recognise the court.' It was reported in the newspapers that he was going to blow up Cammell Laird's shipyard in Birkenhead but in his autobiography he neither confirms nor denies that this was the case. It was often reported that he was on an unauthorised solo mission to England to blow up Liverpool docks, however. The magistrates ascertained that he was 'mute by malice' in the court when he refused to state a plea of guilty or innocent, and so the court entered the plea of 'not guilty' on his behalf. He did, however, deliver a speech which he had learnt by heart: 'By plantation, famine and massacre you have striven to drive the people of Ireland, but in seven centuries you have not succeeded.' The judge regretted he could not sentence him to fourteen years' penal servitude because he was under 18. He could only sentence him to three years in borstal detention (see Chapter Three). In response, Brendan shouted 'Up the Republic!'

Brendan was sent to Feltham Boys' Prison which, as well as being a prison, was temporarily acting as a borstal allocation centre. On arrival there he was placed in the dormitory and was 'glad of the company' after being in solitary at Walton, and there was more food than he could eat. He was also given clothes, including pyjamas which he had never had before. Unlike at Walton, the boys were allowed to chat while at work sewing mail bags. For dinner there was plenty of sea pie or stew (not the cold bully beef they had on Saturdays in Walton but all hot meals). Brendan thought the officers in Feltham were decent and treated him well. However, they did not get much exercise at Feltham but this seemed to be mainly due to overcrowding, and not by design. While at Feltham Brendan and the other inmates were anxious to find out which borstal they were to be sent to. The North Sea Wall and Hollesley Bay were both open institutions. This is where Brendan wanted to go as they were on the sea and 'famous for freedom', open air and hard work. He got his wish. On arriving at Hollesley Bay he remembered that he liked the buildings because they were less like 'a jail than any place could be'. His house had a games room, a library and a gym but he found it very cold at night. His first job allocation was gardening and at first he was excited about the prospect of being outside, but later he asked to be moved to the engineering department, which he was 'more interested in'. He was eventually promoted to painter, which was the job he had wanted all along. He also became a server in Mass, despite being excommunicated. He could not take the sacrament but he could speak Latin and they needed someone.

Before Brendan was sent to a borstal he had written and published pieces in verse and prose in various illegal and semi-illegal republican and left-wing papers and magazines, since he was 12 years old. He was part of the youth IRA. At Hollesley there was a sports day where the staff and all their families attended. On one occasion there was also an essay competition, which Brendan entered confidently and won. His subject was 'the sad and beautiful capital of that sad and beautiful island ...'. His prize was 100 cigarettes. At this special occasion they sang songs, played tug of war and ran races. He describes this memory fondly. Against the rules, they went swimming every Saturday in the summer: 'It was a great summer, and we were sorry in a kind of way to see it finished ... but time past is like a bank balance to a prisoner ...'. Despite life being better in the borstal than at Walton, Brendan does allude to some unpleasantness. For example, one boy was allegedly attacked by an officer in the Part-Worn Stores. He was said to have hit him on the bare backside while he was changing his shorts. On top of this, as time went on his friends were released, and then he got into his first real trouble. He gave his 'dog ends' (cigarette butts) to a prisoner in the 'chokey' (usually a slang term for prison, but Behan uses this term for the solitary confinement cell) and was caught by an officer. This brought him before the governor and he was sent to the 'chokey' himself until the governor decided otherwise.

Finally, the day came for his release from the borstal. A sergeant who took part in the raid which resulted in his arrest said: 'They've made a man out of you, Brendan.' Brendan admitted that, except for his latest difficulty (referring to his solitary confinement), he had been 'well looked after'. He caught the boat to Ireland in 1941, 'for the fair hills of Holy Ireland'. However, this was not the end of his criminal activities. He was arrested in 1942 for attempting to murder two detectives of the Garda Siochana (more commonly referred to as the Gardaí or 'the Guards', the Garda Siochana is the police force of the Republic of Ireland). This time Brendan was sentenced to penal servitude for fourteen years. He served his sentence at Mountjoy Prison and the Curragh Camp. He was released under a general amnesty for IRA prisoners in 1946. All this had happened by the time he was

Brendan Behan. *(Library of Congress Prints and Photographs Division/Wikimedia Commons)*

just 23. He did serve another short prison sentence, in 1947, for helping to break an IRA member out of a Manchester jail. At this point he left the IRA, returned to 'civil society' and married Beatrice Salkeld in 1955. Together they had a daughter, Blanaid, in 1963.

While Brendan's criminal and political activities were an important part of his life, it was not the whole of his life. He became a well-known and disciplined writer and was able to earn a living from his work, although he was also renowned for drinking heavily. His biggest success came in 1954 when his play *The Quare Fellow* was produced in Dublin and eventually ended up in the West End. However, his later books had to be dictated because he was no longer able to write for long periods. He had developed diabetes in the early 1950s and in 1964 he collapsed and later died in hospital aged 41. At his funeral he was given a full IRA guard of honour.

CHAPTER SIX

CONCLUSION

This book has answered a few questions, and raised a few more. There are so many opinions and attitudes towards juvenile crime and youth justice that we seem as far away from solving the problem as the people we have been talking about in this book. At least we have one advantage that they did not possess: a longer perspective. As researchers, we also have more data at our disposal (thanks mainly to digitisation) than historians and researchers have ever possessed. Armed with this knowledge, let's return to some of the fundamental questions we posed at the beginning of the book.

Was 'juvenile delinquency' invented or discovered? The history of this subject cannot be separated from the idea of 'good children' and 'bad children'. We could say that the concept of delinquency grew alongside the growing separation of children from the adult world. Children started to be treated as a special and different group in society from the eighteenth century. They had different leisure pursuits, a period for education (especially for the middle and upper classes), and were removed from the workplace. 'Good children' took advantage of the things that society wanted to give them, and were quiet and grateful. Those children who did not meet the increasingly high standards of behaviour expected of them were looked down upon. The authorities thought that they needed controlling and punishing. However, this was tempered with the idea that children could be turned back to the 'good' side, and 'reformed' into useful members of society. If they could do that, and many of the children we talk about in this book did, then society could accept them again. Those who could not grew into the hardened offenders that society feared most.

A great deal of scrutiny and attention was fixed upon children to see which group they were growing into. The industrial and reformatory school system was an attempt to divert children away from crime, and it seems to have had reasonable success in this aim. The training and education such schools provided did allow their children to find employment or to join the military (with heroic but sad results for many who were sent to military training ships like the *Akbar*).

We have tried to describe the lives of children who underwent different experiences and forms of punishment with sensitivity and using a good ethical approach. This means we have to discuss the recent revelations about the abuse of children 'in care'. Many children who were placed into institutions for their own and society's good (or so it was claimed) have suffered informal and terribly abusive punishments and abuse at the hands of the very people who were supposed to look after them. We have not discovered any evidence of sexual abuse in the lives of the children we discuss, but that does not mean it didn't exist. It would have been ignored, condoned or undiscovered at the time, and therefore not entered into any written document that we can see.

Our belief is that the best way of understanding significant changes in society is by examining the impact they had on individual lives. The case studies given in this book do not encapsulate the whole history of juvenile crime and punishment. Indeed, because we can never know everything about a person's life (only the details that have survived in official documents), we may not have captured every aspect of any of the featured children's lives. However, in every single one we can glimpse something of the motivations that may have provoked offending, such as poor parenting, poverty, opportunity and so on, as well as changes in the punishment and 'reform' of children over time.

As we have said several times in this book, most people have someone in their family line who 'offended' against society, most of whom would have done so while they were young. Some will have never had their indiscretions discovered, and so the crime is lost to the historical record. Some, on the other hand, would have been arrested and prosecuted, and maybe ended up in Van Diemen's Land or a reformatory somewhere. These boys and girls are much more visible to researchers. We know more about the children who broke the law than about those who did not. Historians and criminologists have been able to write broad histories using these sources. However, we still need to understand individual stories in order to get the broadest picture which captures all of the complexities of youth justice and its effects. It is also, of course, intensely rewarding to family historians to discover more about their ancestors, and court and prison records offer some of the best opportunities to do just that.

If you do want to carry out your own research project, and we very much hope that you do, then the records we have discussed might help you, and the books we include in the 'Further Reading' section may aid you even more in putting the information you find into a broader historical context. Good luck!

FURTHER READING

Online sources
Australian Newspapers Online, *Trove*; found at: http://trove.nla.gov.au/newspaper
Barnardo's, *Barnardo's Family History Service*; found at: www.barnardos.org.uk/who_we_are/history/family_history_service.htm
British Library, *The Police Gazette*; found at: http://www.bl.uk/learning/histcitizen/21cc/crime/media1/newspapers1/gazette1/gazette.html
British Newspaper Archive, *19th Century British Library Newspaper collection*; found at: http://www.britishnewspaperarchive.ac.uk/
Children's Homes, *The institutions that become home for Britain's children and young people*; found at: www.childrenshomes.org.uk
Digital Panopticon, *Tracing London Convicts in Britain & Australia, 1780–1925*; found at: https://www.digitalpanopticon.org/
Founders & Survivors, *Founders & Survivors: Australian Life course in Historical Context 1803–1920*; found at: http://foundersandsurvivors.org/pubsearch
Gale, *The Times Digital Archive, 1785–2011*; found at: http://www.gale.com/c/the-times-digital-archive
Hidden Lives Revealed, *A Virtual Archive – Children in Care 1881–1981*; found at: www.hiddenlives.org.uk
London Metropolitan Archives (2011), *London Metropolitan Archives Information Leaflet Number 59 Prison Records*; found at: https://www.cityoflondon.gov.uk/things-to-do/london-metropolitan-archives/visitor-information/Documents/59-prison-records.pdf
Old Bailey Online, 'Punishments at the Old Bailey'; found at: https://www.oldbaileyonline.org/static/Punishment.jsp#corporal
Surrey County Council, *Surrey History Centre*; found at: www.surreycc.gov.uk/heritage-culture-and-recreation/archives-and-history/surrey-history-centre/surrey-history-centre-help-for-researchers/archives-and-history-research-guides/the-royal-philanthropic-school-at-redhill
Tasmanian Government, *Tasmanian Names Index*; found at http://linctas.ent.sirsidynix.net.au/client/en_AU/names/

For people who want to know more about this subject:
Brooke, A. and Brandon, D., *Bound for Botany Bay* (The National Archives, 2005).
Davies, A., *The Gangs of Manchester: The Story of the Scuttlers, Britain's First Youth Cult* (Milo Books, 2008).
Duckworth, J., *Fagin's Children – Criminal Children in Victorian England* (Hambledon and London, 2002).
Johnston, H., Cox, D. and Godfrey, B., *100 Convicts: Life Inside and Outside of Prison* (P&S True Crime, 2016).
Pearson, G., *Hooligan. A History of Respectable Fears* (Palgrave, 1983).
Williams, L., *Wayward Women. Female Offending in Victorian England* (Pen & Sword Books, 2016).

For people who want to become experts in this subject:

Alker, Z. and Godfrey, B., 'War as an opportunity for divergence and desistence from crime, 1750–1945', in Walklate, S. and McGarry, R., *Criminology and War: Transgressing the Borders* (2015).

Beddoe, D., *Welsh Convict Women: A study of women transported from Wales to Australia 1787–1852* (S. Williams, 1979).

Behan, B., *Borstal Boy* (Hutchinson, 1958).

Berlanstein, L.R., 'Vagrants, Beggars and Thieves: Delinquent Boys in Mid-Nineteenth-Century Paris', *Journal of Social History* (2001), pp. 531–52.

Cowley, T., 'Female Factories of Van Diemen's Land', in *Women Transported: Life in Australia's Convict Female Factories*; found at: http://tradecoastcentralheritage-park.com.au/_dbase_upl/women_transported.pdf, pp. 53–69.

Cox, P., *Gender, Justice and Welfare: Bad Girls in Britain, 1900–1950* (Palgrave Macmillan, 2003).

Cox, P. and Shore, H., *Becoming Delinquent: British and European youth, 1650–1950* (Ashgate, 2002).

Elkin, W.A. and Kittermaster, D.B., *The Borstal: A Critical Study* (The Howard League of Penal Reform, 1949).

Fox, L.W., *The English Prison and Borstal Systems* (Nabu Press, 1952).

Foxhall, K., 'From Convicts to Colonists: The Health of Prisoners and the Voyage to Australia, 1823–53', *The Journal of Imperial and Commonwealth History* (2011), 39:1, pp. 1–19.

Gard, R.L., *The End of the Road: A History of the Abolition of Corporal Punishment in the Courts of England and Wales* (Brown Walker Press, 2009).

Godfrey, B., *Crime in England, 1880–1945 – The rough and the criminal, the political and the incarcerated* (Routledge, 2014).

Godfrey, B., Cox, P., Shore, H. and Alker, Z., *Young Criminal Lives: Life Courses and Life Chances after 1850* (Oxford University Press, 2017).

Hood, R., *Borstal Re-Assessed* (Heinemann, 1965).

Hooper, F.C., *'Prison Boys of Port Arthur': A Study of the Point Puer Boys Establishment, Van Diemen's Land, 1834–1850* (University of Melbourne, 1967).

Howard, S., 'Bloody Code: Reflecting on a decade of the Old Bailey Online and the Digital Futures of Our Criminal Past', *Law, Crime and History* (2015), 1.

Johnston, H., *Crime in England 1815–1880: Experiencing the Criminal Justice System* (Routledge, 2015).

Kavanagh, J. and Snowden, D., *Van Diemen's Women: A History of Transportation to Tasmania* (The History Press, 2015).

Mayhew, H., *London Labour and the London Poor*, vol. IV (Wordsworth Editions Ltd, 1861).

Meredith, D. and Oxley, D., 'Contracting convicts: The convict labour market in Van Diemen's Land 1840–1857', *Australian Economic History Review* (2005), 45:1, pp. 45–72.

Radzinowicz, Sir L. and Hood, R., *The Emergence of Penal Policy in Victorian and Edwardian England* (Clarendon Press, 1990).

Shaw, A., *Convicts and the Colonies: A Study of penal transportation from Great Britain and Ireland to Australia and other parts of the British Empire* (Faber, 1998).

Shore, H., *Artful Dodgers: Youth and Crime in Early Nineteenth-Century London* (Boydell Press, 1999).

Shore, H., 'Transportation, Penal Ideology and the Experience of Juvenile Offenders in England and Australia in the Early Nineteenth Century, *Crime, History and Societies* (2002), 6:2, pp. 81–102.

Shore, H., '''Inventing'' the Juvenile Delinquent in Nineteenth-Century Europe', in Godfrey, B., Emsley, C. and Dunstall G. (eds), *Comparative Histories of Crime* (2003)

Slee, J., 'Point Puer unpublished report for Port Arthur Historic Site Management Authority', Unpublished (2003), pp. 1–40.

Stack, J., 'Reformatory and industrial schools and the decline of child imprisonment in mid-Victorian England and Wales', *History of Education* (1994), 23:1, pp. 59–73.

Trepanier, J., 'Juvenile Courts After 100 Years: Past and Present Orientations', *European Journal on Criminal Policy and Research* (1999), 7, pp. 303–27.

Warder J. and Wilson, R., 'The British Borstal Training System', *Journal of Criminal Law and Criminology* (1973), 64:1, pp. 118–27.

Watkins, E.D., 'Juvenile convicts and their colonial familial lives', *The History of the Family* (2018) (available at: https://doi.org/10.1080/1081602X.2017.1417882).

Watkins, E.D., 'Transported Beyond the Seas: Criminal Juveniles', in J.E. Baxter & M. Ellis (eds), *Nineteenth Century Childhoods in Interdisciplinary and International Perspectives*, Series: Childhood in the Past 6 (Oxbow, 2018).

Watson, J., 'Reformatory and Industrial Schools', *Journal of the Royal Statistical Society* (1896), 59:2, pp. 255–317.

INDEX